Praise for FRAGMENTS OF GOLD:

"Being a ministry leader for more than 40 years, I am delighted to view these fragments. Years ago, these fragments were presented to us as a *holy garment* from the Lord as a covering to bring HIM glory. But when societal ways and ideas infiltrated church life, ministry leaders became distracted and these fragments were dislodged from the garment we were given. The Old Testament priests had an outer garment that displayed…*fragments of gold* in the book of Exodus 39. I pray that God's blessings continue to fall on Pastor K. J. Butler and Bishop J. Brice. *"To God be the Glory for the recovering of the GOLD!"*

        Pastor Melynn Murphy
        The Spirit of the Lord Gives Life Ministries, Inc.
        Paterson, New Jersey

"Maybe your excuse was: 'I don't know how to!' Pastor Karen lovingly put it all together in one place to avoid leaving you in doubt of 'how to' or 'What do I do?' May **Fragments of Gold** help you in your strive to achieve a *crown of gold* in ministry."

        Reverend J. C. Griffith, Senior Pastor
        The International Deliverance Sanctuary
        London, England

"To the authors of **Fragments** I would like to state that we find the book very informative, full of knowledge and instructions that will assist in the building of the Kingdom of God not only in the lives of young leaders, but also in the lives of the lay members of the body of Christ. We believe that the information given within these pages will help to assist and establish order in the church of our Lord Jesus Christ."

        Pastors Christopher and Tonya Thorton
        Victory in Christ Ministry
        Highland Park, Michigan

"If effective Church leadership has always perplexed you, this book is the key to undo such complications. **Fragments of Gold** offers a biblical guide to the responsibilities of leaders called to do Christian ministry. It will be enormously helpful to those called to the position of assistant pastor, deacon, elder, missionary, teacher, and board member."

        Naomi Rawlings, Associate Pastor, Nurse Educator
        Basseterre Church of God
        St. Kitts, West Indies

"We thank God for inspiring Bishop Brice and Pastor Butler to write ***Fragments of Gold***. It is wisdom for God's leaders of today. Its self-examination and preparation scriptures are to the point. We congratulate Bishop Brice and Pastor Butler."

>Pastor Harmon and Elder Arlene Holden
>Bethel Pentecostal Church
>Bridgeton, New Jersey

"Thank you to Bishop Brice and Pastor Butler for writing ***Fragments of Gold***. This book gives practical tools to navigate through the ups and downs of ministry. We would recommend all novice and seasoned ministers/leaders to read ***Fragments of Gold*** as a source of information and encouragement. No stone has been left unturned!"

>Pastor Hartley and Elder Katherine Pernell
>St. John Holy Church
>Cedarville, New Jersey

"This book is a treasure chest for Christ followers. Karen Butler and Johnny Brice have given us a concise, practical, and biblical guidebook for leadership."

>John D. Peck, Pastor
>Bethel Assembly of God
>Lincoln Park, Michigan

"Authors Karen J. Butler and Johnny Brice have certainly set the standard for practical foundational information for those called to do ministry work. Their ability to search the sacred scriptures captured God's heart. ***Fragments of Gold*** was developed to produce character and sharpen gifts related to ministry. As a leader, I would recommend ***Fragments of Gold*** to be used as a tool of reference for all clergy. Thank you Pastors for your obedience to the Lord to help advance His Kingdom."

>Bishop Kamia White, Senior Pastor
>Reviving Souls Ministries
>Cocoa Beach, Florida

"And you shall know the truth and the truth shall set you free" [John 8:32]. We have a mandate from God to give people "truth." Elder Butler and Bishop Brice have undertaken this task. This book will be a blessing to the Body of Christ. It is a strong Word; it is meat and not milk! It is a Word that will prepare us for the coming of Jesus Christ."

>Elder Leroy Harris, Pastor and Musician
>Waves of Glory Church
>Williamstown, New Jersey

FRAGMENTS of Gold

"A word fitly spoken is like apples of gold in pictures of silver. As an earring of gold, and an ornament of fine gold, so is a wise reprover upon an obedient ear." Proverbs 25:11-12

Wisdom and Word for God's Servant Leaders

KAREN J. BUTLER
AND JOHNNY BRICE

Wings of Deliverance Transforming Ministries
Lincoln Park, Michigan

Fragments of Gold: Wisdom and Word for God's Servant Leaders
©2013 Karen J. Butler and Johnny Brice

All rights reserved.
ISBN 978-0-9911618-8-1

Contact info:
    Elder Karen Butler
    wingsofdeliverancetm@yahoo.com

    Bishop Johnny Brice
    jbrice56@yahoo.com

Publisher:
    Wings of Deliverance Transforming Ministries
    P. O. Box 1342
    Lincoln Park, MI 48146

All Scripture Reference and Research Sources:
    Thompson Chain Reference Bible Special Centennial Edition, KJV, B.B. Kirkbride Bible Company, Inc., Indianapolis, Indiana USA 2007

    The New Strong's Exhaustive Concordance of the Bible, James Strong LL.D, S.T.D. Thompson Nelson Publishers, Nashville, Camden, Kansas City published in Nashville, Tennessee 1990 by Nelson, Inc. Publishers and distributed in Canada by Lawson Fulle. Ltd.

    Merriam-Webster's Dictionary and Thesaurus 2006 by Merriam-Webster, Incorporated.
    Made in the United States of America 13PIT:WCB10 ISBN 978-0-87779-851-4

Editorial and "sack" art by: Karen J. Butler/ Proofing: ProofreadingPal.com

Cover design and interior pre-page layout by LaTanya Orr, Selah Branding and Design LLC, Detroit, MI • www.iselah.com

Final design format by www.sixpennygraphics.com

Printed in the United States of America

Dedications

There are several people we wish to honor in the dedication of this book. We give glory and honor to God for salvation through the blood of Jesus Christ and for choosing us to pass on these fragments of Wisdom and Word to the next generation of servant leaders. We pray that in these sacks of gold they will find instruction that will equip them to better serve as they prepare mankind for the second coming of the Lord.

We are indebted to those who nurtured and trained us; honoring all who had a part in preparing us as servant leaders. Our teachers and tutors include people such as our earthly mothers and grandmothers, spiritual mothers and fathers in the gospel who, under the direction of the Holy Spirit, helped to mold and shape us through instruction, reproof, correction, and rebuke.

First, we want to humbly bow in submission to the passing of, and give honor to, Bishop Brice's mother, Mrs. Martha Ann Greene, who went home to be with the Lord as we were working on the completion of this book. Like my mother, she is a part of the foundation of the Bishop's knowledge and love for Jesus Christ. Though they will miss her, the family takes joy in knowing that one day they will see her again. We know that she would have been very proud of this project in which her son has taken part. We dedicate this book to her and all the siblings, family and friends near and far, and to the memory of his deceased grandparents: Andrew and Irma Witherspoon.

Secondly, to Bishop's lovely wife, Elder Glenda Brice: Thank you for sharing this great man of God with the world and especially with me, your sister. Thank you to Samuel and Arielle, for sharing your father with us.

People do not know how much families sacrifice when their loved ones are involved in ministry. I thank all three of you for loving me, trusting me, and allowing your husband and father to work with me in ministry. Most definitely, I owe you this one. So yes, I dedicate this book to you!

There are a host of others that include deacons, church mothers, auxiliary heads, great musicians and choir directors, associate ministers, family, friends, and other pastors too numerous to name who have left their fingerprints on our hearts. Each person instilled values within us, whether basic or complex, that helped to make us the servant leaders we are today. Individually and collectively they instilled within us Wisdom and Word that is even more precious than gold, for which we are eternally grateful. Though we cannot name them all, we must honor some of our former pastors. And though they have passed on, they left undeniable marks on our lives.

We dedicate this book in memory of two of Bishop's former pastors, Bishop Leonard R. Williams and Pastor Allene Gilmore, and two of mine, Bishop Ruth E. Satchell and Reverend Robert W. Davis. These anointed leaders loved, nurtured, imparted wisdom and trained us while we served as members of their churches in central and southern New Jersey. There were others, but these four not only shared fragments of wisdom, they themselves were as pure gold. Much of the wisdom we gained through their instruction, correction, and rebuke is the reason why we are still standing today, and why we strive for excellence in ministry. We honor their memory by dedicating this book to their families.

We also dedicate this book to Wings of Deliverance Transforming Ministries, Johnny Brice Ministries, Covenant Partners Fellowship Conference, all the former members of Miracle Temple Church of Deliverance, and to those everywhere who have been an encouragement to our ministries. I give special honor to Bethel Assembly of God and Pastor John Peck in Lincoln Park, Michigan whose unconditional love and support made completing this project so much easier.

To those who have encouraged Bishop and me through this project and some difficult times in our lives, I call you church mothers, sisters, brothers, and just plain good friends: Mother Elsie Partida, Brother Raymon Chapman, Mother Lillie Richmond, Mother Lillie Moton, Evangelist Arlene Curvin, Mother Rose Halsey, Pastor Mary Panich,

Pastor Jeanie Williams, The Tate and Dockery family, Brother Kevin Chester, Mother Elsie Burk, Sister Fonda Hale, Elder and Mrs. Armel Sykes, Evangelist D. Gaines, Pastor Melynn Murphy, Dr. Linda St. Martin, Mrs. Doreica (Pinky) McCall, Ms. Cheryl Pierce, and Ms. Cheryl Street. Ok, now I am tearing up!

This book is specifically dedicated to my entire family, first in memory of my grandparents, Mr. and Mrs. Joseph Butler and his sister, my aunt, Mother Lossie Randall (deceased), who served as the National Mother of the First Born Church in Waycross, Georgia, and Bishop Helen Lewis (cousin, deceased), who was the chief overseer of The Church of The Living God, Pillar and Ground of the Truth. Love, honor, and kisses to other living relatives including: Aunt Carol, Uncle Nat, Aunt Ruthie, Nathan, Lori, Kelly, Sumiko, Tara, Cousins Ann Bascom, and Bishop Kamia White; and all the Butlers from Waycross, wherever they may be.

I honor all of those on the Middleton side, including Pastor Willie J. Fletcher (New Jersey) and family, Bishop Meharry Lewis (Alabama); all of my cousins, Mary, Jacqueline, Arlene, Audrey; and all of the children and grandchildren of Clara, Alma, Nathaniel (Buddy), Catherine, and Virginia (all deceased). I love you all!

I dedicate this book to the memory of my father, Deacon Edward Miller (deceased), my paternal aunts and uncles, my sister, Ruth, my brothers Daryl and Wallace, and my cousins Tyrone, Irene, Vanessa, Gilbert, Nita, and Nette, even those I haven't met on the eastern shore of Virginia. I love all of you!

I honor my mother, Mrs. Geraldine Butler, one of the most intelligent and gifted women on the planet. Momma, you and "Grand mom," Mrs. Clara M. Butler (deceased), prepared me to become a woman of God at an early age. You taught me to pray while she showed me how to pray, worship, and praise. You both encouraged me to love God with all my heart and soul. Thank you for the gifts that you passed down, which includes a love for music, and teaching me church administration as well and how to behave myself wisely in the house of the Lord. Mom, thank you also for teaching me to make full use of a dictionary. Not only did you encourage me to find the true meaning of words, but also the meaning of life. For all of this I love you.

Last, but not least, I honor my wonderful son, Geramie, and my new daughter-in-law Mary. I dedicate this to both of you as well. My son, we have been through a lot together, and thank God we survived it! Your mere existence made a huge difference in the woman I was meant to become. You have encouraged your mother in a way that no else could. I hope that I have made you as proud as you have made me. I don't have much according to the world's standards, however I hope that I have and will continue to give you the best inheritance a mother could give, precious sacks of "***Fragments of Gold***." I love you, Mom.

With love and heartfelt thanks to all…Pastor Karen J. Butler

The Fragments of Gold
HALL OF FAME

"Honoring the memory of those gone on who shared "the gold," through Word, Wisdom, Leadership, Music or Love"

Bishop Ruth E. Satchell, NJ	Elder Melva Corley, NJ
Mr. and Mrs. Joseph (Sonny) Butler, NJ	Elder Louis Gordon, NJ
Mother Lossie Randall, GA	Evangelist Mabel Smith, NJ
Deacon Edward Miller, NJ	Elder Curtis Lewis, NJ
Mr. and Mrs. Joe (Sonny) Butler, NJ	Elder Walter Spain, PA
Rev. Robert W. Davis, NJ	Elder Gracie Brantley, NJ
Bishop Mary E. Jackson, PA	Elder John Drysdale, MI
Bishop Annie Chamblin, VA	Evangelist Josephine Leach, NJ
Bishop James Bell, NY	Evangelist Georgia Villegas, NY
Bishop Amy B. Stevens, DE	Sister Doris Als, NJ
Bishop Leonard R. Williams, NJ	Deacon Walter Martin, NJ
Bishop Charles Stevens, DE	Mrs. Ernestine Eady, PA
Bishop William Pugh, PA	Mr. Forrest Hodges, NJ
Bishop Josephine Jones, DE	Mrs. Ida M. Williamson, NJ
Bishop Helen Parker, PA	Elder Easter Mae Farrar, NJ
Bishop James F. Brown, VA	Apostle Willie McCoy, IL
Bishop Lillian Bagley, PA	Deacon & Mother Colquitt, IL
Elder Lila Sparks, FL	Brother Kevin Walker, PA
Andrew and Irma Witherspoon, SC	Min. Rudolph (Ricky) Porterfield, NJ
Bishop Helen Lewis, FL	Mrs. Dorothy Hall, NJ
Elder Anthony Pitts, NJ	Mrs. Doris Walker, NJ
Elder Kezia Agard, PA	Deacon Jesse Ellis, MI
Mother Martha A. Green, NJ	Sister Nell Hunter, NJ
Deacon Timothy Conley, MI	Brother Robert Street, NJ
Mr. Joseph L. McMobley, MI	Sister Marie Bowen, NJ
Deacon Carl Milbourne, NJ	Sister Shirley Kish. MI

The Fragments of Gold
WALL OF FAME

Honoring those who continue to share 'the gold,' through Word, Wisdom, Leadership, Music or Love"

Bethel Pentecostal Church, NJ	Brother Nate Bandy, NJ
Union Baptist Temple, NJ	Evangelist Lenore Gardenhire-Young, NJ
Zion Holy Church, NJ	Evangelist Cynthia Johnson, NJ
St. John Holy Church, NJ	Reverend Lester Taylor, NJ
Trinity Holiness Church, NJ	Ms. Lydia Cleaver, MI
Bishop Helen O. Gillis, VA	Pastor Fred Whitmore and Family, MI
Gilmore Tabernacle Look and Live Ministry, NJ	Bethel Assembly of God, MI
	Minister Lisa Hooks, TN
Mt. Sinai Holy Churches of America, Inc., Int'l.	Evangelist Earlie Butler, GA
	Dr. Cassandra Watson Jones, PA
The First Born Church, GA	Pastor Daryl Parham, NJ
Church of God in Christ, Int'l.	Pastor Arthur (Artie) Parham, NJ
Assemblies of God, Int'l.	Pastor Eleanor Steward, NJ
Pastor Alcides Holguin, MI	Pastor & Mrs. John O. Parker Jr., NJ
Memorial Tabernacle, MI	Sister Wanda Burnside, MI
Bishop Carolyn Ann Webb & GET, NJ	Sister Laura Jones, AL
Apostle Eugene Smith, MI	Sister Lennis Height, MI
Pastors Eustace & Naomi Rawlings, WI	Evangelist Vicky Byrd, MI
Pastor Willie J. Fletcher, NJ	Tabernacle Baptist Church, NJ
Cecil Tabernacle, NJ	Brother James Faison, NJ
Ms. LaTanya Orr, MI	Sister Beverly Peyton-Tinsley, PA
Ms. Deb Tremper, VA	CHRISTNET, MI
TCT Network/WDWO-TV18, MI	Brother Wayne Magee, NJ
Dr. Garth and Tina Coonce, IL	Brother Michael Pernell, NJ
Detroit Panel of "Ask the Pastor," MI	Cornerstone Family Worship Center, MI
Bishop Stanley Edwards, VA	Elder and Mrs. Larry Twyman, DC
Elder Minnie Lincoln, NJ	Elder Florence Pugh, VA
Faith Tabernacle Church, NJ	Pastor and Mrs. Everett Thomas, MI
Assistant Pastor Helena P. Reid, PA	Pastor Luz Vallejo, FL
Pastor Sylvia Slaughter, NJ	Heart for Him Ministries, MI
Pastor Dean Staley, NC	Blessed Hope Church, MI
Brother Michael Lamb, MI	

Introduction

"And thou shalt teach them ordinances and laws, and shall shew them the way wherein they must walk, and the work that they must do." —Exodus 18:20

Bishop and I conversed over the phone about the fact that many of today's servant leaders have not had the benefit of receiving the gold nuggets of wisdom that we had received from great leaders. Reflecting on our lives, we realized that preparation for leadership of excellence came under tutors such as our parents, teachers, members of the laity, and anointed ministers of music as well as our pastors. Excitement was in our voices as we discussed the wisdom we had gained under great men and women of God. The Spirit of the Lord gave us an unction to record the wisdom we had gleaned and the idea to write a book blossomed. We thought: "Perhaps we could share with others some of the precious gold that we had inherited."

In these perilous times we need to pull together and mentor those who will serve as prophets and priests of the "LAST DAY." When you know who you are in Christ, one who is truly called of God, you don't mind mentoring your successor, as it was with Elijah and Elisha as written in 1 Kings 19:16–21 and 2 Kings 2:1–15. The desire to help, train, mentor, and encourage is in our hearts.

In the first meeting Bishop and I shared our notes as we recalled years of experience in church work. Both of us had ministered in the Word, administration, and in music. We were surprised at the years of wisdom we had gained. One night as I compiled the notes, I heard the title "Fragments of Gold." Later the Holy Spirit clarified it with a subtopic: "Word and Wisdom for God's Servant Leaders." I thought, "Wow, God, you are awesome!" Little did I know that I was about to endure a difficult challenge in the birth of this idea. However we both knew that the end result would be well worth it.

We worked over the phone and in person until the hand of God clarified these decrees for the Body of Christ. God used Pastor Melynn Murphy (you will find her endorsement in the earlier pages) to confirm this endeavor by expounding on the gold in Exodus 39:1–3. It had to be beaten into pieces in order to weave it into the priest's garment of service. Consequently, I can't think of a better way to end this introduction than to say that we hope you will do the same. Weave these fragments into your spiritual garment of service so that you can bring great glory to God through the manner in which you serve His people. Now go and find your sack of gold!

DISCLAIMER

Though we have written this book to be a blessing to the entire Body of Christ, we do recognize differences in church doctrine, structure, and leadership. Therefore we respect the responsibility of each leader to decide whether these fragments comply with the teachings of their ministry. With the exception of taking responsibility for any textual error that may have occurred due to human oversight; we take no credit for the effect this book may have on the Body of Christ. We do however accept full responsibility for our obedience to the confirmation of its publishing by the Holy Spirit. All glory and praise however goes to Almighty God and we are confident that He will make full proof of this ministry. Amen!

Instructions

If you have been praying and asking the Lord for wisdom, find Wisdom and Word in these sacks according to your calling, title, or position in ministry. Each sack (chapter) is numbered to help you find the section that refers to your area of service. Each fragment has an identifying number to make it easier to reference whether for personal study or instruction. All of the fragments have at least one scripture as it relates to its meaning. Please note: The individual books of the Bible are separated by semi-colons; if different chapters are in the same book, they are listed with colons and commas, like this example: [Psalm 34:1–3, 47:1, 51:1–12, 95:1–3]. However, all verses are separated by commas only. It may appear as though some fragments have been repeated and this was done purposely to make sure that the message is fully understood for each area of ministry. Read the fragments under the guidance of the Holy Spirit and allow Him to confirm it. Apply those fragments to your *garment of service*, and endeavor to bring great glory to God!

"The King James Version translation will be used throughout this book."

CONTENTS

Sack One ~ 1
DEFINING THE CALL OF A SERVANT LEADER

Sack Two ~ 8
REFINING THE SERVANT LEADER

Sack Three ~ 32
ENHANCING THE SHEPHERD LEADER/OVERSEER

Sack Four ~ 56
REFINING THE EVANGELIST/MISSIONARY

Sack Five ~ 64
CLARIFYING THE RESPONSIBILITIES OF AN APPOINTMENT

Sack Six ~ 72
REFINING THE MINISTERS OF MUSIC

Sack Seven ~ 81
REFLECTIONS OF GOLD

Portraits ~ 86
ABOUT THE AUTHORS

Sack One
DEFINING THE CALL OF A SERVANT LEADER

(For those newly called or assigned to servant leadership)

1. Take a self-inventory by asking a few questions: "Am I saved and sanctified? Have I been delivered? Am I filled with the Holy Ghost?" There is no need to go any further in this book if you cannot answer these questions with an honest "yes!"

> ▶ 2 Corinthians 13:5; 2 Chronicles 5:11; Acts 1:8;
> Acts 19:1–8; John 3:16–17, 20:22; Luke 24:49.

2. What event took place that persuaded you of your call?

> ▶ 1 Samuel 3:4–19; Acts 9:1–16.

3. Prayerfully examine whose voice, word, command, or request you heard that thoroughly convinced of your call to the ministry.

> ▶ Exodus 3:5–6, 9–15; Joshua 1; Acts 9:1–20.

4. Know your primary mission.

> ▶ Matthew 4:19, 28:19–20; Luke 4:18–19, 5:10b;
> Acts 1:4–8.

5. Prayerfully examine what type of calling, gift, or appointment in which you are to operate. Have you been called, gifted, or appointed to be a prayer warrior, intercessor, missionary, deacon, prophet, preacher, evangelist, minister, teacher, elder, pastor, apostle, overseer, psalmist, or church worker? Either way you look at it, they all mean that you are a servant!

> ▶ Ephesians 4:11–12; Matthew 23:11–12.

6. Bow down and count up the cost!

> ▶ Luke 14:25–33.

7. Make preparations for your role in ministry. Find out what the responsibilities are for the call you are accepting.

> ▶ 2 Timothy 2:15, 4:5; Ephesians 4:10–12;
> 1 Timothy 3:1–7; 1 Corinthians 12:4–31.

8. <u>STOP RUNNING!</u> Stop making excuses and accept God's will and destiny for your life!

> ▶ Exodus 4: 10; Jonah 1; Esther 4:10–16; Jeremiah 1:4–10.

9. Upon your conviction and confirmation of your call from the Lord, humbly accept by responding affirmatively with an eternal "yes," "I will," "I'll obey," "send me," etc. (Satchell 1976–1999).

> ▶ 1 Samuel 3:1–21; Isaiah 6; Jonah 1.

10. Pray and seek God's guidance as to whom you should make your confession. You should be a member of a church under a spiritual covering; you cannot expect others to follow you if you have not been an humble follower.

> ▶ 1 Samuel 3:8–20; Joshua 14:7–9; 1 Kings 19:20–21.

11. Share the call with someone with experience in the field who is led by the Spirit of God, such as your pastor, who can also serve as a mentor.

> ▶ 1 Samuel 3; Acts 9:1–18.

12. Ask yourself if you have been faithful to God and to your own local ministry!

> ▸ Matthew 25:20–23; 1 Corinthians 4:1–2; Psalm 101:6.

13. Humble yourself and listen to what your leader or mentor has to say, as they are led by God, and then take it to the Lord in prayer for confirmation.

> ▸ 1 Kings 19:20–21; 1 Samuel 3:8–9, 16: 7–13; Proverbs 3:6–7.

14. WAIT ON YOUR CALLING! Wait for God's timing and His ordained season for you to go forth in ministry.

> ▸ Ecclesiastes 3:1–11, 17; Romans 12:7; Habakkuk 2:3.

15. Be mindful of the governing rules of your church or its organization pertaining to releasing new ministers, such as a waiting period before licensing or ordination, initial sermons, or your release to preach.

> ▸ Hebrews 13:7; Acts 14:23, 16:4–5; 1 Timothy 2:7; Titus 1:5.

16. Be warned, not everyone is going to believe or accept your call, nor be happy for you.

> ▸ Genesis 37:1–11; Matthew 13:57–58; Acts 9:21–26.

17. Step up your devotion and prayer time—you are going to need it! Fasting, whether from food, media, or other distractions, are just some of the ways to deny the flesh while waiting to hear from God.

> ▸ Daniel 6:1–10; Mark 1:35; Luke 2:37, 6:12.

18. When you pray, check your spirit for possible hindrances, such as unforgiveness, bitterness, doubt, pride, haughtiness, and especially unconfessed sins.

> ▸ Jonah 4; Psalm 51, 69:5, 139:23; Lamentations 3:40;
> 2 Corinthians 4:1–2, 13:5; Ephesians 4:30–32; 1 John 5:17.

19. REPENT! When there are areas in your life in which you know that you have not completely yielded, you should ask the Lord's forgiveness and set things in order.

> ▸ Psalm 51; Luke 13:5; Romans 3:23, 8:1–2, 12:1–3.

20. Make sure that you did not misinterpret the call.

> ▸ 1 Samuel 3; Proverbs 2:6, 4:7; Esther 5:9–14, 6:6–12.

21. Make sure that you do not misrepresent your call.

> ▸ 2 Corinthians 4:5, 11:13–15; Ephesians 4:1–3; Proverbs 25:6–8.

22. Endeavor to understand the elements that comprise your ministry.

> ▸ Exodus 3:11–13; Colossians 1:25; Luke 4:18.

23. Be committed to studying the Word of God daily. Hopefully you will always operate in the spirit. However, it is necessary to have some type of teaching, experience, or formal education in the Word.

> ▸ 2 Timothy 2:15, 3:16–17; John 14:26.

24. Are you being led by God or being pushed into ministry by family or friends?

> ▸ Proverbs 25:6; Matthew 20:21–23.

25. Don't allow yourself to be pushed too fast by anyone; this is God's business and He is the one who has ordained when, where, how, and even what He's called you to do.

> ▸ Psalm 31:15; Proverbs 25:6–8; Ecclesiastes 3:1; Habakkuk 2:3.

26. Don't move too slowly out of fear and miss the season God has chosen for you.

> ▸ Esther 14b; Ecclesiastes 3:1–8; Colossians 1:25; 2 Timothy 1:6–8.

27. Don't be afraid or intimidated, the call is not about you; it is about God's purpose, and His purpose usually involves souls.

> ▶ Psalm 56:3, 118:6; Joshua 1:5–9;
> 2 Corinthians 4:1–5.

28. Always follow God's lead!

> ▶ Exodus 3:12–16; Proverbs 3:5–7; Isaiah 48:17.

29. Learn the difference between your calling and your assignment.

> ▶ Exodus 3:4–9, 10–12; Jonah 1:2; Acts 9:6, 15–16.

30. Walk in the integrity of your calling but always wait on your assignment!

> ▶ Psalm 25:21, 27:14.

31. Be reminded that there will be hindrances!

> ▶ 1 Thessalonians 2:18; 1 Peter 5:8–9.

32. Do you have the true concept of the Gospel and what role you will play pertaining to it?

> ▶ Romans 1:16; John 3:16–17.

33. Do you love all of God's people (races, genders, and ages) or would your ministry be tainted by prejudice?

> ▶ John 3:16–17; Acts 10:28–35, 19:34;
> Galatians 2:12; 1 John 4:7–12; Jude 1:21–23.

34. Ask yourself if having celebrity or worldly status as a minister is important to you.

> ▶ Genesis 11:4; Isaiah 14:13.

35. Decide whether or not you could operate in ministry if there is no money involved because in most cases, money will not be involved!

> ▶ 1 Peter 5:2; Proverbs 15:27; Acts 5:20.

36. Don't use ministry to chase after rainbows (worldly success). Rainbows are a manifestation of a covenant with God!

> ▶ Genesis 9:12–16.

37. Ponder whether or not you can stand being persecuted for your beliefs.

> ▶ Matthew 5:11; 1 Corinthians 4:10–14;
> 2 Corinthians 12:10; 2 Timothy 3:12.

38. Do not expect to *be* served, but *to* serve!

> ▶ Mark 10:43–44; John 13:12–16, 21:16.

39. Are you willing to make sacrifices as well as suffer?

> ▶ Acts 16:22; Philippians 3:9–10;
> Hebrews 13:13–16; 1 Peter 2:25, 3:17.

40. Could you accept an assignment that would require you to relocate?

> ▶ Genesis 12:1–4; Acts 18:1–11, 28:1–12.

41. Consider whether or not you could accept an assignment in a foreign field.

> ▶ Matthew 9:37, 28:19–20; Mark 16:15–20.

42. PRAY FOR THE ANOINTING!

> ▶ Isaiah 10:27; Luke 4:18; 1 Corinthians 1:21–29;
> 1 John 2:27–29.

43. Do not be intimidated by your age; God can use whomever He wishes. Consider people like Moses, who performed some of his greatest exploits at an older age. Josiah ruled a kingdom at the age of eight, and Timothy served as a pastor at a young age.

> ▶ Deuteronomy 34:7; Joshua 14:10–12; 2 Kings 22:1;
> 1 Timothy 4:4–12; 2 Timothy 1:1–15;
> 1 John 2:13–14; John 8:55–59; Luke 2:36–37.

44. Don't be intimidated by your gender; the Lord calls and uses those He desires. He calls women to the ministry just as he does men. In the spirit there is no gender. Consider even a judge and prophetesses of old. God used them for His glory and honor and He can use you. Women in ministry should never try to prove their calling by disrespecting their male counterparts nor attempting to act (minister) like them. Yokes are destroyed because of the anointing and not because of gender!

> ▶ Judges 4:1–5; 2 Chronicles 34:21–28; 2 Kings 22:14; Joel 2:28–29; Isaiah 10:27; Luke 2:36; Acts 2:17–18; Galatians 3:28.

Sack Two
REFINING THE SERVANT LEADER

(Associate ministers, evangelists, pastors, apostles, prophets, teachers)

45. Reexamine your call and consider your commitment to the Lord as well as the assignment. Are you humbled by this call? If the answer is "yes," then that is a good sign! However, if you are not committed to it, leave it alone!

> ▶ Luke 9:57–62; Hosea 10:2; 1 Timothy 6:20a;
> 1 Corinthians 9:16–19; 1 Kings 18:21; James 1:8;
> Colossians 1:25–29.

46. Do you have a covering? Are you affiliated with a local church and its leader? Have you been a faithful member?

> ▶ Colossians 2:6–7; 1 Timothy 5:17; Hebrews 13:7.

47. Before you minister to someone else, how do you treat your family members, such as your spouse, children, parents and other family and friends? Will your treatment of them bring swift criticisms of reproach upon your call to ministry?

> ▶ 1 Timothy 3:2–5–6; 1 Timothy 5:8; Joshua 24:15.

48. When pondering the call, those who are married should consider that their spouse can help to make or break their ministry and that they will experience the highs and lows of it along with them. Perhaps you should consider this before you say "I do," or "I will."

> ▶ Numbers 18:1; Job 2:9–10; 1 Corinthians 7:33–34;
> Colossians 3:16–25.

49. Husbands, do you love your wives as Christ loves the church? You have a responsibility to honor and respect your wife even if she is not a minister herself. She is there to support you in ministry and should be respected as your helpmate. Be a godly example for your members.

> ▶ 1 Peter 3:7; Genesis 2:23–24; Ecclesiastes 9:9;
> Ephesians 5:23–25; Colossians 3:18–19.

50. If you are a married female minister/leader, do you respect and honor your husband as the head of your home? Your ministry cannot be effective by disrespecting your husband, even if he is not yet saved. Be a godly example for your members.

> ▶ Judges 4:4–5; Proverbs 31:27–28; Ephesians 5:22–33;
> 1 Corinthians 7:1–16; 1 Peter 3:1–9.

51. If you are single, then abide in your calling; pray for contentment in whatever state God allows you to dwell. Wait on God and allow Him to connect you with the right mate according to His will so that there will be no hindrance to the ministry He has assigned to you.

> ▶ Proverbs 3:5–6; 1 Corinthians 7:8–9, 32–33;
> 2 Corinthians 6:14–18; 1 Timothy 6:6;

52. Consider, acknowledge, confess and make amends for any prior sins committed or negativity you've created that will shroud your ministry if it is not corrected.

> ▶ Jeremiah 7:3–7; 1 Corinthians 11:28;
> 2 Corinthians 13:5–8; Psalm 32:5;
> James 5:16; 1 John 1:8–10.

53. Dedicate yourself to the Lord and to His work through study, fasting, and prayer.

> ▸ Matthew 26:39; 2 Chronicles 17:16; Acts 6:4; Romans 12:1–2.

54. Learn to accept divinely inspired counsel from your spiritual leader pastor/overseer.

> ▸ Proverbs 12:15, 15:32; 1 Timothy 1–2.

55. Get to know your place in ministry and walk in that anointing.

> ▸ Ephesians 4:1–12.

56. Make sure that you have a Word from the Lord for His people and not a sermon you have copied from someone else.

> ▸ Jeremiah 23:30, 37:17b; Hebrews 5:13–14; John 5:38–39; Deuteronomy 12:32.

57. Always remember to study and pray before you preach.

> ▸ 2 Timothy 2:7–15; Isaiah 34:16; John 5:39.

58. Remember: a sermon is the <u>teaching</u>, <u>expounding</u>, and <u>proclamation of the Gospel</u>; a testimony gives evidence. Know the difference! Exercise wisdom when using testimonies.

> ▸ 1 Corinthians 9:16; 2 Corinthians 4:5; 2 Thessalonians 1:10; John 5:39; Acts 5:42.

59. Familiarize yourself with proper protocol in ministry, such as opening prayers or invocations, exhortations, offertory prayers, prayers of thanksgiving, prayers of benediction, as well as prayers for the sick and shut-in, prayers of repentance, and intercessory prayers, including those dealing with demonic activity.

> ▸ Psalm 34:1–3, 47:1, 51:1–12, 95:1–3; Psalm 100, 103:1–5; 1 Thessalonians 3:11–13; Ephesians 3:20–21; James 5:13–15; John 11:41–42, 17:1–26; Philippians 4:7; 1 Peter 5:10–11; Jude 1:24–25; Mark 5:1–16; Acts 12:4–16, 16:16–18; 1 Timothy 2:1–3.

60. Learn the proper way to minister in different settings, such as weddings, funerals, hospitals, nursing homes, and prisons so that you glorify God, edify His people, and avoid breaking rules or causing any legal ramifications.

> ▸ Romans 13:1–8; Titus 3:1; 1 Peter 2:13–17.

61. Learn how to carry out the ordinances and order of the church, such as presiding over a service, calling the congregants to order, serving communion/feet washing, baptism, consecration, dedication services, and conducting business meetings.

> ▸ Luke 22:9–20; Matthew 26:19; John 13:1–17;
> 1 Corinthians 11:23–34.

62. Learn how to give speeches/remarks of edification to a bereaved family during a funeral (brief words of comfort if you are not there to preach the eulogy), and at a function of honor (relate to the honoree and not anything or anyone else). Do what you are asked to do unless otherwise unctioned by the Holy Spirit or those in charge.

> ▸ Ecclesiastes 5:1–2, 3:1–7; Romans 15:16;
> 1 Corinthians 14:26; 2 Corinthians 1:4.

63. Never conduct yourself in an unseemly manner. Avoid embarrassing yourself, and bringing reproach on the church and the name of Jesus Christ.

> ▸ Psalm 101:2; Ecclesiastes 5:12; 1 Timothy 3:15.

64. Take the time to evaluate your behavior during the worship service as well as in the Lord's house and in His work. Do you respect His works? Is your business and talking on your cell phone more important to you than respecting the Lord's house and ministering to His people? Is it easy for Him to get your attention or would He have to vie or wait for it?

> ▸ Matthew 21:13a; 1 Corinthians 11:20–22;
> Philippians 3:17–19, 4:9; 1 Peter 5:1–3;
> 1 Timothy 4:12; Titus 2:7–8.

65. Would others be inspired to respect and honor God by your example and commitment to Him?

> ▶ 1 Timothy 4:12; Titus 2:7–8.

66. Take every opportunity to serve and learn from your leaders. Heed their examples or their formal instruction.

> ▶ 2 Timothy 2:2; Philippians 3:17.

67. Be still and wait on God to advise you of the location (city, state, country, area) where He wants you to serve.

> ▶ Proverbs 3:5–7; Genesis 12:1–3; Isaiah 48:17.

68. Be patient and wait on the Lord for the clarity of your assignment.

> ▶ Psalm 40:1, 106:13.

69. Consider the credentials necessary for the office you have been called to and have accepted. This should be discussed with your pastor.

> ▶ 1 Corinthians 12; Colossians 4:17; Ephesians 4:11–12; 2 Timothy 4:5; Titus 3:1.

70. Familiarize yourself with the documents required for your type of ministry, such as state rules for performing marriage ceremonies or a passport for ministry abroad. Do not perform any type of ceremony or other procedure without the proper credentials.

> ▶ Colossians 4:17; Titus 3:1; Romans 13:1–8.

71. Remember that no licensing, certifications, or degrees will make you a better minister—they only help you to be more prepared, especially when it comes to the proper protocol in the world.

> ▶ 2 Corinthians 3:5–6.

72. Don't be hung up on titles. Let the life you live and the service you give define who you are and the respect you should receive.

> ▶ 2 Timothy 4:5; Job 32:21–22; Matthew 23:5–11.

73. Know that if you do not take your call seriously, no one else will. The call of God on your life and the anointing are very serious!

> ▸ Isaiah 10:27; 1 Corinthians 1:20–22.

74. Please do not wear clergy attire—unless you are led by God or if it is mandatory per your leader or religious affiliation—especially if you do not understand its significance. It is not necessary to prove that you have been called!

> ▸ 1 Samuel 17:38–39; 2 Timothy 4:5; Matthew 23:1–11.

75. Learn to dress appropriately (per your church's requirements) for the different types of ministerial occasions at which you will be present. There were strict guidelines regarding dress under the law for the priests in the Old Testament scriptures. However, in this modern day, at least be clean and formally dressed for such occasions as weddings and funerals. Avoid any attire that will complicate the task to which you've been assigned. Do not destroy your witness! Use modesty and temperance in all things. Your outward appearance should reflect your inward commitment to the service and public witness of Christ and your personal regard for His people.

> ▸ Exodus 28:1–7; 1 Corinthians 1:8–9; Philippians 4:5;
> Galatians 5:1–23; 1 John 2:15; Ecclesiastes 9:8;
> 1 Timothy 2:9–10.

76. Continue to examine yourself daily for any hindrances to your assignment whether it is you, someone else, or any spirit that has been assigned to block you.

> ▸ Nehemiah 4:8; 1 Thessalonians 2:18.

77. Be reminded that you were not just appointed by man to carry out this assignment because you were liked, but that you have been anointed by God. Being charismatic is wonderful but it won't last; you must have more!

> ▸ 2 Samuel 14:25, 15:1–16; John 12:43.

78. WARNING: This 21st Century is highly pressurized! Can you handle the pressure?

> ▶ 2 Timothy 3:1–7.

79. Get to know those who labor among you; this is critical in ministry!

> ▶ 1 Thessalonians 5:12.

80. Again, before operating in ministry, please take self-inventory. Check for any roots of bitterness in your heart. Bitter fruit can later manifest and thereby destroy your effectiveness and credibility.

> ▶ Ephesians 4:29–32; Hebrews 12:14–17.

81. Avoid ministering beyond your experience unless under the influence of the Holy Spirit. Learn to stay in your lane. Preach, teach, sing, and demonstrate the way God has equipped you, and not like someone else.

> ▶ Jeremiah 23:30; 1 Timothy 3:6; Hebrews 5:12;
> 1 Peter 4:11.

82. BE AUTHENTICALLY YOU! PLEASE DON'T BE A PHONEY!

> ▶ Leviticus 19:11; Psalm 119:104–118;
> Titus 1:16; Isaiah 57:4; Jeremiah 17:9.

83. Do not accept the call for the love of money!

> ▶ 1 Timothy 6:10; Titus 1:11.

84. Be reminded that you have been called to serve God and His people!

> ▶ Galatians 5:13; 2 Peter 2:15–16; 1 Peter 5:1–3.

85. Keep the call in perspective; you make full proof of your ministry.

> ▶ Matthew 5:16; 1 Peter 2:12–16; 2 Timothy 4:5.

86. Should you err from the truth, repent quickly by acknowledging your sin, confessing and turning away from it as you ask the Lord's forgiveness.

> ▸ Psalm 51; 2 Corinthians 7:10; 1 John 1:9; Luke 15:18.

87. Make confession as often as necessary! Avoid covering you sin. Pray about whether or not it is an offense that should be brought out in the open to avoid future threatening, blackmail-type attacks from the enemy and bringing reproach on the church or your personal ministry. Consider those involved and whether confession to them, such as spouses or family members, should be made and/or an open apology. Humble yourself and make amends so God can deliver you and help you to go on with your ministry. Be led by the Spirit and not your flesh.

> ▸ Ezra 10:11; Jeremiah 3:13; Joshua 7:20; 1 Samuel 15:24;
> 2 Samuel 12:13; Luke 15:18; Proverbs 28:13; James 5:16;
> 1 John 1:9; Matthew 5:22–25.

88. Guard the anointing over your life; avoid all things, including people and your own disobedience that you will strip you of it!

> ▸ Matthew 26:41; Judges 16:18–20; 1 Samuel 16:14.

89. Don't be pushy or greedy, your season will come; wait your turn.

> ▸ Proverbs 15:27; Isaiah 56:10–11; Ecclesiastes 3:1.

90. All ministries are to be carried out in the spirit of love. Seek God for a double portion of His unconditional love.

> ▸ 1 Corinthians 13:1–8; Song of Solomon 8:6–7;
> Galatians 5:22.

91. DO NOT PROMOTE YOURSELF! Wait for promotion or elevation from God. Stay focused! The devil will use those you least expect to get you off track.

> ▸ Psalm 75:4–7; Proverbs 3:35.

92. Remember, your primary purpose and goal is SOULS, SOULS, SOULS! This is your priority and it pleases the heart of God.

▸ Matthew 9:37; Proverbs 11:30; Luke 4:18.

93. Take nothing for granted; pray and consult God about everything. Pray always!

▸ Isaiah 55:6; Jeremiah 29:11–14; Luke 18:1.

94. Don't be angry when or if God changes His mind! Remember that God is sovereign!

▸ James 1:19–20; Jonah 1–4; Ecclesiastes 7:9; Ephesians 4:26; 2 Chronicles 20:6.

95. Understand that failure can sometimes be experienced on the road to success. Use your failures as stepping-stones and your successes as pearls of humility. Wisdom gained is a combination of the two.

▸ Romans 8:28; Joshua 1:6–8.

96. Push past your fears and only trust God's ability in you! Remember: timidity will stifle, cripple, and hinder your progress and/or development in advancing in Kingdom dimension.

▸ Matthew 25:24–30; 2 Timothy 1:6–7.

97. Let your inner conqueror out!

▸ Romans 8:37.

98. Practice walking by faith and not by sight.

▸ 2 Corinthians 5:7.

99. Keep thine own self under subjection.

▸ 1 Corinthians 9:27.

100. Never mock or criticize a fellow clergyman.

▸ Psalm 22:6–9; Acts 2:12–21; Jude 18–19; 2 Chronicles 36:16; Nehemiah 4:1.

101. Be a true worshipper of God; you certainly can't admonish anyone else to if you don't!

> ▸ 2 Chronicles 7:3; John 4:23–24.

102. Learn to respect both calm and exuberant forms of worship in different cultures, as people are led by the Spirit of God. It will help you to become a more well-rounded leader.

> ▸ 1 Samuel 1:11–13; 2 Samuel 6:14–16;
> Psalm 150, 84:2–4; Luke 19:37.

103. Be moved with compassion for God's people.

> ▸ Matthew 14:14–21, 20:34; Mark 1:41;
> Luke 7:13–14; Proverbs 19:17.

104. Constant lateness is not an example of good stewardship of God's time. Prepare to be on time, and when you aren't, humble yourself to explain and/or apologize. Are you always late to your job as well? If you have no justifiable reason for consistent tardiness, then perhaps you should occupy a seat and pray until you learn how to be a better steward of the Lord's time.

> ▸ Ecclesiastes 3:1, 17; Psalm 89:47, 102:11;
> Matthew 25:1–13; Luke 14:11; 1 Peter 5:5–6; 2 Peter 3:8;
> Romans 13:11; Proverbs 26:13–16; Hebrews 6:12.

105. Be a leader who will give from your lack as well as your abundance.

> ▸ Acts 4:34–35; Mark 12:42–44.

106. Never seek fame and fortune in serving God's people.

> ▸ Matthew 6:19–34, 23:5–11; Romans 12:16; Genesis 11:4.

107. Always seek the welfare of God's people.

> ▸ Jeremiah 38:4; Romans 12:13; 2 Corinthians 10:18, 11:28.

108. Know that it is a privilege to have the anointing of God over your life.

> ▶ Proverbs 8:32–36; Luke 1:30; 2 Corinthians 10:18; 1 John 2:27.

109. Never assume that you have figured God out and that you know Him better than others.

> ▶ Isaiah 55:8–9; Job 38; Romans 11:23.

110. Do you intend to help build the Kingdom of God or a kingdom for yourself? Do not behave as Absalom did by trying to steal what you think is a kingdom that has not been assigned to you.

> ▶ Genesis 11:1–4; Proverbs 19:21; Jeremiah 22:13–14;
> 2 Samuel 15:1–6; Romans 2:21–23.

111. A wise leader will consider that he is the least among his fellow clergymen.

> ▶ Romans 12:16–18; Philippians 2:3–4; Matthew 11:11.

112. Never think more highly of yourself than you ought to.

> ▶ Romans 12:3–4, 16; Galatians 6:3;
> Proverbs 26:12; 1 Corinthians 8:1–3.

113. Never seek to divide or stir up strife anywhere among God's people.

> ▶ Philippians 1:15, 2:3; James 3:6; Proverbs 20:3.

114. Always sanctify the Lord before His people.

> ▶ Isaiah 5:15–16, 8:13.

115. Avoid making vain and negative statements before God's people.

> ▶ James 4:14–17; Jeremiah 23:15–28, 28:15;
> Numbers 13:25–33.

116. Respect every pastor and that church's pulpit.

> ▶ 1 Thessalonians 5:11–13; 1 Peter 2:13–17.

117. Learn to respect all positions along with those who rule over you.

> ▸ 1 Peter 2:13–17; Romans 12:4; Hebrews 13:7, 17.

118. Never allow yourself to be jealous or intimidated by someone else's calling or gift.

> ▸ Songs of Solomon 8:6; Proverbs 6:34; Hebrews 13:5; 2 Peter 2:14; 2 Timothy 3:3.

119. Be an advocate of peace and respect all people regardless of race, culture, or gender.

> ▸ Mark 16:15–20; Zechariah 2:11; John 4:9; Acts 10:34; James 2:3, 9.

120. Always speak the truth especially since you are serving "The Truth."

> ▸ Colossians 3:9; John 14:6; Ephesians 4:25.

121. Respect leaders in the secular world, which includes those in government.

> ▸ Romans 13:1–8; 1 Peter 2:13–17; Titus 3:1.

122. Learn to speak or be quiet as you are led by the Holy Ghost.

> ▸ 1 Thessalonians 4:11; Ecclesiastes 3:7; John 16:13; 1 Corinthians 2:13.

123. Strive for integrity every day in your personal life as well as in your ministry.

> ▸ Numbers 16:15; Proverbs 20:6–7; 2 Corinthians 6:3–10.

124. Pray for the spirit of discernment—you are going to need it!

> ▸ 1 Kings 3:9; 1 Corinthians 2:12–14; Hebrews 5:14.

125. Learn when to take a stand and when to walk away.

> ▶ Ecclesiastes 8:3; Romans 1:15–16, 8:14, 16:17; Galatians 2:7–11; Philippians 1:17, 27, 4:1; Acts 23:11–24; 1 Peter 5:8–9; Titus 1:10–14; 1 Corinthians 16:13.

126. Make great effort to be a peaceable leader, one that is easy to entreat.

> ▶ Hebrews 12:14; Romans 12:18.

127. Practice the law of reciprocity daily, whether it is in finances or general giving.

> ▶ 2 Corinthians 9:6–8; Matthew 5:42; Luke 6:38.

128. Though you may not walk a mile in the other man's shoes, do mark the shoes that man has walked in. Take heed to the example whether it was good or bad.

> ▶ Psalm 37:37; Romans 16:17; Philippians 3:17–18.

129. Remember that intercession is an integral part of your ministry.

> ▶ 1 Timothy 2:1–3; Exodus 32:31–32; Numbers 12:13; Acts 7:59–60, 12:5–12; 1 Samuel 7:5; Job 42:10; Psalm 106:23; John 17:1–26;

130. Commit to being a leader who is dedicated to visiting the sick and shut-in, those who are incarcerated, grief stricken, and those who are in need. Hospital visitation should be brief, polite, and effective. Talk faith and not doubt, speak life not death, consider the feelings of the family. Absolutely no loud noise is appropriate at any time.

> ▶ Matthew 25:35–36; James 5:13–15.

131. Covet no one else's property, including their spouse.

> ▶ Exodus 20:17; Ephesians 5:3; 2 Samuel 11:2–5.

132. Know that leadership is not an opportunity for you to manipulate God's people.

> ▶ Jeremiah 5: 31, 23:11–14, 30–32; Hosea 4:6–9;
> Matthew 27:20; Mark 15:11.

133. Make sure that you are not an idol-worshipper.

> ▶ 1 John 5:21; 1 Corinthians, 8:4–6, 10:6–11.

134. Surround yourself with people you can trust to help strengthen your ministry, people who will tell you the truth.

> ▶ Psalm 119:63; Proverbs 11:14, 13:20, 15:22, 32.

135. Glorify God and edify His people.

> ▶ 1 Corinthians 6:20; Matthew 5:16;
> 1 Thessalonians 5:11; 2 Corinthians 12:19.

136. Humble yourself to hear wise instruction from your elders or those who are more experienced than yourself.

> ▶ Exodus 18:14–24; 1 Kings 12:6–15.

137. Young ministers, never push your elders aside, wait your turn; they just might out-live you!

> ▶ Psalm 37:25, 71:18; 1 Peter 5:1–5;
> 1 Timothy 5:1–3, 17–21; Proverbs 22:28–29;
> Ecclesiastes 3:1.

138. The elders and youth alike must respect each other.

> ▶ 1 Timothy 4:12, 5:1–3; Titus 2;
> Lamentations 5:12–16; 2 Kings 2:23; Proverbs 23:22;
> Job 32:6; Ephesians 6:1–4; 1 Samuel 17:26–51.

139. Make sure that you have been delivered before trying to deliver someone else.

> ▶ Matthew 15:14; Luke 4:18; 2 Corinthians 5:17.

140. Upon entering a pastor's pulpit, quietly acknowledge God by bowing your head in prayer and discreetly acknowledging your fellow clergymen perhaps with a nod and/or later, a handshake. If you are late, do not enter the pulpit at all except when you are summoned or are given permission by the pastor.

> ▸ Philippians 2:3–8; Proverbs 22:29, 25:6–8.

141. All leaders, no matter what their gender, should always give respect to their counterparts! No matter what you have been taught about men or women in ministry, respect is the key. God gets no glory out of us publicly humiliating or disrespecting anyone.

> ▸ Judges 4; Acts 17:12; Romans 12, 13:7;
> Galatians 3:28; 1 Timothy 1:5, 5:17; Titus 2:3.

142. All ministers should be dressed appropriately when sitting in the pulpit. Females, no dresses that are too short; males, make sure that there are no rips or tears or any such things that would expose private areas. Don't make it difficult for people to hear God's Word.

> ▸ Romans 14:13; Isaiah 57:14; 1 Timothy 2:9–10;
> 1 Peter 3:3–5.

143. Never approach an altar to pray for souls without clearance from the leader of that ministry. This applies whether you belong to that church or not and especially if you are a visitor.

> ▸ 2 Timothy 2:24–26; Romans 13:7, 14:12–19;
> 2 Thessalonians 5:12.

144. Learn to pray effectively around the altar with souls. Pray without unnecessary yelling and physically trying to push people to the floor to make it appear as though your prayer has caused them to be slain in the spirit. The Holy Spirit can do His own work!

> ▸ Proverbs 4:5, 11:30; 1 Samuel 19:21–24.

145. Learn to be watchful around the altar: "Just as the Spirit of the Lord is there, there can also be demonic activity." Learn to protect God's people without stifling their free worship. (Sparks 1977–1998)

> ▶ 1 Peter 5:8; Proverbs 11:30;
> 1 Thessalonians 5:19; 2 Corinthians 3:17.

146. Prayerfully learn how to discern between hearts that are seeking God and spirits that are trying to draw attention away from the move of God.

> ▶ 1 Corinthians 2:10–14; 1 Kings 3:9; Hebrews 5:14.

147. Use caution when you lay hands on members of the opposite sex at the altar or otherwise, without witnesses being present.

> ▶ 1 Corinthians 6:12; 1 Thessalonians 5:22.

148. Avoid counseling a pastor's members without their awareness and approval. Certain circumstances may differ but be under the direction of the Holy Ghost.

> ▶ Isaiah 30:1; Hebrews 5:12–14; Philippians 1:9–10.

149. Never preach in your church or anyone else's without prior permission from your pastor and the pastor of the other church. Honor all leaders.

> ▶ Romans 13:7.

150. Avoid taking a pastor's members (especially those who are scheduled to serve in their church that day) with you to personal ministry engagements without the pastor's knowledge. You may not be knowledgeable of that person's level of spiritual maturity and therefore risk exposing them to hindrances.

> ▶ 1 Corinthians 14:32–33, 40, 15:33;
> Exodus 34:12; 1 John 2:10.

151. Never prophesy in a church without first being unctioned by the Holy Ghost, being released by God, and by following the order in that ministry as directed by the pastor.

> ▸ 1 Corinthians 14:32–33, 40.

152. Learn the difference between confrontation and contention, and pray about how to deal with each situation.

> ▸ Acts 15; Proverbs 3:30; Isaiah 1:18; 2 Timothy 2:14; Philippians 2:3–4; Jude 1:3; Ecclesiastes 7:25.

153. Learn to be discreet. Make sure that people and God can trust you with things that should not be discussed with others.

> ▸ James 1:26; Proverbs 11:9, 13:3.

154. Mark the example of your leader if you have a good one, or one that is not, so that you can learn what kind of leader to be or not to be.

> ▸ Matthew 4:19; John 12:26; Philippians 3:16–18.

155. Humble yourself and allow God to handle an offense from another leader. Make sure that you are not the one at fault, and if so that you do your part to make it right.

> ▸ Acts 15; Matthew 5:23–24.

156. Remember to allow the Holy Ghost to teach you as well as your education and experience, when it comes to the things of God.

> ▸ 2 Kings 22:14; 2 Timothy 2:15, 4:5; John 14:26.

157. Though God's word and the calling on your life are very serious, learn how to laugh and also enjoy the life God has given you. You will be more of a blessing to God's people.

> ▸ Psalm 126:1–3; Proverbs 17:22.

158. Be affectionate toward God's people and not affectionately lustful.

> ▸ Romans 12:10; Colossians 3:5–6; James 2:12–16.

159. Allow your gift to make room for you and not you or anyone else to make room for your gift. When it comes to ministry, God is the only agent you need.

> ▸ Proverbs 18:16; James 1:17; 1 Corinthians 14:12.

160. Study when you do not have to preach so that you will be ready when you do.

> ▸ Psalm 1:1–3; 2 Timothy 2:15, 3:16–17, 4:14–16.

161. As an associate minister, remember that the pastor may allow you to minister in that ministry, but that congregation is not your charge. (Satchell 1975–1999)

> ▸ 1 Timothy 1:18; 2 Timothy 4:1–3; 1 Corinthians 16:15–16.

162. Avoid leaving a ministry without clearance from God. A proper oral or written statement of resignation is always appropriate. At all cost, leave peacefully so that your ministry will continue to be blessed.

> ▸ Hebrews 12:14; Romans 12:18; 1 Kings 19:9;
> Jonah 1:3–4; Proverbs 27:8.

163. Never stand up in a church without the leader's clearance and announce that you are leaving that ministry. It is not your responsibility to enlighten the members of that congregation.

> ▸ Proverbs 13:3, 21:23; Hebrews 13:7; 1 Timothy 5:17.

164. Cover your pastor or the one who is in charge, as did Jonathan with David, but not as a partaker in any leader's sin.

> ▸ 1 Samuel 18:1–4, 20:4; Exodus 17:10–12; 2 Samuel 24:1–4.

165. Remember; you may be a leader or have a title, but that is not a license for you to physically or spiritually assault or abuse God's people. Be mindful of the fact that God is always watching even if men aren't.

> ▸ Psalm 10:14, 11:4; Proverbs 15:3;
> Acts 5:27–42; Ezekiel 34:1–10.

166. Remember, improper and inordinate behaviors will not only cause people to lose confidence in your ministry but will also bring reproach on the Gospel of Jesus Christ and the Baptized Body of Believers, which includes your own local ministry.

▸ Hebrews 12:1; Ezekiel 23:11; Colossians 3:5–9.

167. Mark an abusive leader and you will learn what type of leader God has not called you to be. Unfortunately there are some who desire the office only for the perceived authority and power they wish to exercise to manipulate God's people. Kindness, if shown at all, is shown only when it benefits their plans. Allow God to handle this type of leader.

▸ Romans 16:17–18; 1 Samuel 24:3–7; Acts 23:5.

168. Learn how to wait on God, yet without being complacent.

▸ Psalm 25:5, 27:14, 123:2; Isaiah 40:31; Proverbs 20:22.

169. Earnestly contend for the faith!

▸ Jude 1:3.

170. All rebuke, reproof, and correction should always be done in the spirit of love.

▸ 2 Timothy 4:2; Proverbs 10:12; Romans 13:10; 2 Corinthians 5:14; Galatians 6:1.

171. Learn to persevere. There are many things that will not happen overnight.

▸ Ephesians 6:18; Galatians 6:9; Philippians 3:13–14.

172. Respect diversities of ministry such as prosperity, healing, deliverance, and missions as they are all for the edifying of the body of Christ and for the building up of the "Kingdom of God." Strive for balance in ministry.

▸ Romans 12:3–6; 1 Corinthians 12.

173. Never try to panhandle or prostitute the gospel. Do not use it just as a way to get money. Those who labor in the gospel are worthy of hire, but wisdom must be used in how it relates to finances and material wealth.

> ▶ 2 Kings 5:20–27; Matthew 21:12–13; 1 Timothy 5:18.

174. Never allow anyone to prostitute your ministry (use it strictly for gain), not even you! Be careful that your "gain," is not "filthy lucre."

> ▶ 1 Samuel 8:3; Acts 8:17–24, 16:16–20;
> 1 Timothy 3:3, 8; Titus 1:7, 11.

175. When working with other leaders, place differences aside for the benefit of God's people in obedience to the will of God.

> ▶ Philippians 2:3–1–14; Titus 3:9; Isaiah 1:17–19.

176. Always give the utmost respect and honor to the leader you serve under and their congregants.

> ▶ 2 Kings 2:1–15; 1 Corinthians 12:23–26;
> Galatians 6:10; 1 Timothy 5:17; 1 Peter 2:17;
> Hebrews 13:1–7; Acts 23:5;

177. Arrogance in a servant leader is absolutely appalling! Humble yourself so God won't have to. Allow Him through others to commend you on your works.

> ▶ Proverbs 16:18, 27:1–2; Isaiah 2:11; Matthew 23:12.

178. Take a stand for the Word of God, but in the spirit of love and without hatred!

> ▶ 1 Timothy 6:12; Romans 1:16; Jude 1:3.

179. Operate in a spirit of excellence in things pertaining to the mind, body, and soul.

> ▶ Proverbs 14:34; Philippians 1:9–10, 3:8; 1 Corinthians 14:12.

180. Present yourself in a spirit of cleanliness in the natural as well as in the spirit.

> ▸ Isaiah 1:16; Psalm 51:7–10, 73:1; Matthew 6:17; Romans 12:1–2; 1 Corinthians 6:19–20; Exodus 19:14.

181. Keep your breath fresh and your body clean, as you offer a word of prayer or counsel to God's people. They will respect you for it.

> ▸ Romans 12:1–2; 1 Corinthians 6:19–20; Matthew 6:16–17.

182. Profanity is always unacceptable; it reveals your denial of Jesus. It takes a more intelligent and wise human being to know how to express themselves without the use of perverse communication.

> ▸ Matthew 26:74–75; Exodus 20:7; Leviticus 19:12; Proverbs 10:32; Ecclesiastes 12:9–10; Malachi 2:6–8.

183. Be careful who you share your personal, private business with, they can use it against you later. And furthermore, is it glorifying to God for them to know it?

> ▸ Proverbs 13:3; Psalm 118:8–9; Proverbs 11:13; Judges 16; Micah 7:5.

184. Ask the Lord to put a watch over your tongue daily.

> ▸ Psalm 141:3; James 1:26; Proverbs 10:19–21, 21:23; 1 Peter 3:10.

185. Say what God says, about you and His people. If God says something is blessed then it's blessed, but if he says it is cursed, then it is cursed!

> ▸ Proverbs 18:21; 1 Kings 22:13–20; Luke 1:20–23, 57–64; Jeremiah 26:2–7; Matthew 5:1–12.

186. Avoid rude behaviors such as being unfriendly and disrespectful.

> ▸ Proverbs 8:13, 15:28, 16:7, 18:24, 27:10; Ecclesiastes 4:9–10; 1 Corinthians 13.

187. Ask God to help you to behave wisely.

> ▶ Psalm 101:2; 2 Thessalonians 3:6–7; James 3:13;
> 1 Samuel 18:14–15.

188. Avoid sexual misconduct in any form!

> ▶ 1 Samuel 2:22–25; 1 Corinthians 5:1–9, 6:13–20;
> Romans 1:26–29; 2 Corinthians 12:21.

189. Be careful not to usurp authority. Never take authority over anything that has not been designated to you.

> ▶ 2 Samuel 15:1–6; Matthew 28:18; 1 Peter 3:22;
> Hebrews 13:17; Proverbs 29:2.

190. Don't give to be seen, but please be seen giving both tithes and free-will offerings. Give due benevolence.

> ▶ Matthew 5:42; Luke 6:38; 2 Corinthians 9:6;
> Malachi 3:10; Isaiah 58:10; Mark 12:42–44; Acts 20:35.

191. Do not steal whether it is God's tithes and/or offerings, other people's money, or even their ideas.

> ▶ Exodus 20:15; Romans 2:21.

192. Avoid using gimmicks to persuade God's people to give money. The Word of God is powerful enough to motivate them. When you teach God's people obedience to the Word of God "freely giving" becomes a joy!

> ▶ Acts 4:31–37, 20:35; 2 Corinthians 8:1–21, 9:6–7; Luke 21:1–4.

193. Be a faithful and wise steward over all things.

> ▶ Matthew 25:1–13; Luke 12:42–48;
> Ephesians 5:15–17; Colossians 4:5–6.

194. Be honest in your business as well as your religious dealings.

> ▶ Proverbs 19:1, 20:7, 22:29; 2 Kings 12:7–16;
> Acts 5:1–11, 6:3; Romans 12:17, 13:8.

195. Faithfulness is a key to good success in your ministry, but avoid operating in a take-over spirit.

> ▸ Matthew 25:23, 26:7–10, 26:51; Romans 10:2;
> Luke 18:15–16; 2 Samuel 15:1–6; Mark 10:13–14, 14:47–49.

196. Do not trust your own flesh as well as anyone else's!

> ▸ Romans 7:18–25, 8:1–13; Psalm 118:8–9;
> Philippians 3:1–9.

197. When considering the removal of toxic things and people from your life, consider whether or not you are toxic to someone else as well.

> ▸ Hebrews 12:1; 1 Corinthians 11:28; Romans 8:1;
> Amos 3:3; Proverbs 4:14–16, 26; Matthew 7:1–5, 12, 21–23.

198. Learn the power of humility in apologizing and making amends.

> ▸ Psalm 51:3–4; Luke 15:18–24, 18:13–14.

199. Remember, that you may be in head leadership one day, so don't expect others to follow you when you have not followed your leaders.

> ▸ Joshua 1; 1 Peter 2:17–21; Romans 13:1.

200. Never seek to destroy anyone nor their influence. God sees and knows all!

> ▸ Jeremiah 16:17; Proverbs 11:9, 15:3;
> Acts 6:11–15; Psalm 31:13; Mark 4:22.

201. NEWS FLASH: Suffering can help you to be a better leader.

> ▸ Philippians 1:12–21, 3:9–10; Acts 5:40–41;
> Romans 8:28; 1 Peter 5:10.

202. Reminder: Your primary mission is souls, and your responsibility is to work with and assist those who have the same mission!

> ▸ Matthew 4:19; Luke 5:6–10; Daniel 12:3;
> 1 Corinthians 9:19–27; Proverbs 11:30; James 5:20.

203. Always remember that as an associate minister or other leader, you too are responsible for bringing in as well as ministering to souls. Sheep beget sheep, meaning "birth." What? Isn't the ministry where you are a member good enough to share with your family and friends? If your answer is "no," then why are you there? Hopefully you are not there just to get a title, papers, recognition, or validation!

> ▸ Proverbs 11:30; Matthew 9:37–38;
> John 4:35–38; Acts 16:15, 33–34.

204. Be aware, that vices should be avoided! Addictions such as smoking, drinking, drugs, sex, and gambling will ruin your witness! If you are engaging in these activities it is because you have not yet been delivered from a nature of carnality. Though you may have been called, your true purpose is being thwarted by your flesh, consequently giving the enemy control over you and your ministry. Diligently seeking deliverance from this type of bondage, humbling yourself and admitting you have a problem would be one of the first steps to your victory. A period of restoration or time off from serving can be beneficial in getting your mind and spirit back on track and in line with the Will of God. If you won't do it for yourself, do it for others.

> ▸ Romans 6; Psalm 34:18; 2 Corinthians 5:17;
> Galatians 5; Ephesians 4:17–30, 5:1–10;
> Jude 1:4–19; Romans 8:1–16.

Sack Three
ENHANCING THE SHEPHERD LEADER/OVERSEER

(Pastors, bishops, apostles, etc. those with a flock/congregation)

205. Through much prayer and consecration make sure that it is the will of God for you to operate in this calling and at this level of ministry.

> ▶ 2 Corinthians 3, 4, 6:1–10; Ephesians 3:7–11;
> John 21:17; Acts 20:28, 26:16; 1 Peter 5:2.

206. Are you a sanctified, consecrated vessel for the Lord?

> ▶ 2 Chronicles 5:11; Acts 9:15, 13:2–5;
> 1 Thessalonians 5:23, 4:4–7;
> Romans 9:21; 2 Timothy 2:19–21.

207. Wait on God to tell you where he wants you to shepherd and when He will send or lead you to the sheep that he has ordained to follow you. This can happen by assignment and/or appointment.

> ▶ Romans 12:6–7; Acts 26:16–18; Ephesians 3:1–11;
> 2 Timothy 4:11–12; Hebrews 1:14.

208. Make sure that you are shepherding your own family before you try leading others.

> ▶ 1 Timothy 3:4–7; Joshua 24:15.

209. Pray for the anointing!

> ▶ Luke 4:18; 1 John 2:20–27; 2 Corinthians 1:21–22.

210. Saturate yourself in God's Word through personal study or a formal education.

> ▶ 2 Timothy 2:15; Psalm 119:9–20, 97–105; Acts 6:4.

211. Make sure that you have bona fide and proper credentials from a legitimate organization or educational institution and not just from the Internet. This is advisable for the purposes of doing business with the secular world and primarily because you are dealing with the lives of God's people.

> ▶ Colossians 4:17; 1 Peter 2:13–17;
> 2 Timothy 4:5; Galatians 6:4–6.

212. Make sure that you are not a novice and that you have had teaching and/or experience in spiritually leading God's people.

> ▶ 1 Timothy 3; Romans 12:3–8; 1 Peter 5:5.

213. Know your ministry. You are not only a fisherman, now you have become a shepherd. Your responsibilities have broadened. You will now lead, feed, teach, nurture, protect, counsel, and oversee as well as comfort those whom God has assigned to your hand.

> ▶ Matthew 4:19, 28:19–20; 1 Corinthians 9:13–23;
> Jude 22–23; Acts 20:28; Luke 4:18–19;
> 1 Thessalonians 2:4–14; 1 Timothy 4; 2 Timothy 2:14–26.

214. Give and/or get an understanding from the beginning. Does this church belong to you or to the Lord? Does it belong to you personally, paid for with your money and is considered to be a piece of the inheritance for your children or family members? Please make everyone aware of that from the establishment of the church so that your associate leaders will not overstep their bounds by thinking that they would be eligible to be the future pastor when you are gone.

> ▶ Proverbs 4:7, 16:8, 21:6; Psalm 101:7;
> 1 Thessalonians 4:6; Colossians 3:9–10.

215. Word of advice: Don't try to scale the fish before you get them in the boat! Be patient and don't try to force people to change overnight.

> ▸ 1 Corinthians 3:1–2; 2 Corinthians 5:17;
> 1 Thessalonians 5:14.

216. Though your ministry is considered independent, is there someone over you to help you keep your spiritual inventory? Make yourself accountable to someone!

> ▸ Romans 14:12–18; James 5:16; Matthew 18:23; Hebrews 13:17.

217. Do yourself and everyone a favor by remembering that you are human and just a servant and not the people's God!

> ▸ Exodus 20:3, 34:14; 1 Corinthians 10:22–24; Matthew 23:12.

218. Don't shorten your days by trying to be a god; don't take glory from God!

> ▸ Acts 10:25–26, 12:21–23, 14:11–19; 1 Corinthians 3:21–23.

219. Purpose in your heart to do Kingdom building and don't try to build a kingdom for yourself.

> ▸ Matthew 11:12, 28:19–20; Ezekiel 34:2–3; Isaiah 56:11.

220. Consider what your true motive is for saying "yes" to the call of "shepherd?"

> ▸ Ezekiel 34:2; 2 Corinthians 4:1–15.

221. Do not despise small or large assemblies (churches). Remember, this is the church of the living God and not a corporation that you are building in order to make a great name for yourself.

> ▸ Psalm 127:1; Micah 7:1; Matthew 18:20;
> Acts 2:41, 5:38–42, 16:13.

222. Don't make the habit of comparing your ministry to someone else's.

> ▸ 1 Corinthians 4:6–20; Luke 22:24–27; John 5:40–44.

Enhancing the Shepherd Leader/Overseer

223. Never compete with other pastors or their churches. The work of the Lord is not a competition!

> ▶ 1 Corinthians 4:1–9; James 4:1–18; Luke 22:24;
> Proverbs 25:8; Galatians 5:26.

224. Never put down other ministries by bragging and/or gossiping.

> ▶ 2 Corinthians 5:10–13, 10:12–18;
> Proverbs 20:6, 30:12–17.

225. Whether you have church in your house (a small number) or in a cathedral (a large number), be faithful by loving and taking care of the sheep.

> ▶ Acts 4:31–35, 20:28; 1 Corinthians 16:19;
> 2 Corinthians 8–9; Micah 7:1; Colossians 4:15.

226. Love one member as much as you would love one thousand. Don't give up if your membership decreases. Until the Lord directs you to shut down, you are still responsible for those souls.

> ▶ Matthew 18:5–13, 20; Micah 7:1–7;
> 1 Peter 5:2; Acts 20:28.

227. Your ministry may be classified as independent, but remember the work of the gospel is a collaborative; you are a part of the Body of Christ! We are in this thing together!

> ▶ 1 Corinthians 3:3–13; Judges 20:11; Ephesians 4:1–7.

228. Testify! The people need to hear where the Lord brought you from and what He has done in your life. You cannot make others believe what He can do, if He has never done anything for you.

> ▶ Acts 22:1–15, 26:1–22; 1 Corinthians 2:1;
> Revelation 12:11.

229. Ask yourself if you can be faithful serving without a salary, offering, a day of appreciation, accolades, or even a "Thank you?"

> ▶ 1 Corinthians 4:10–13; 2 Corinthians 12:10–19;
> Luke 17:11–18; 2 Thessalonians 3:8–10; Hebrews 6:9–10.

230. Be mindful of the people but according to the will of God. God is in control; don't allow people to control you, not even those with money!

> ▶ 1 Samuel 15:20–26; 1 Peter 5:2–4; Proverbs 22:2; 2 Timothy 6:17; Romans 6:16; 2 Peter 2:15.

231. Love and respect the people that God gives you even if you don't like things about them!

> ▶ 1 Peter 5:2; Acts 20:28; 1 John 3, 5:2.

232. You must have and exercise faith daily!

> ▶ 2 Corinthians 5:7; Hebrews 11.

233. Learn to sanctify God before His people.

> ▶ Numbers 20:12; Isaiah 8:13; Psalm 29:2, 107:32; 1 Peter 3:15.

234. Get to know co-laborers in the Body of Christ. Fellowship will cultivate relationships.

> ▶ 1 Thessalonians 5:11–13; Acts 2:42–47; Romans 1:12.

235. Never pit members against one another by showing partiality or respect of persons.

> ▶ Leviticus 19:13–18; Job 13:10; 1 Corinthians 8:12; 1 Timothy 5:21; James 2:1–16, 3:13–18.

236. Never force your members to involve themselves in something in which you don't actively participate, such as praying, fasting, self-denial, or sacrificial giving. Show them by your lead.

> ▶ 1 Timothy 4:11–16; Titus 2:7–15.

237. Never allow your members to see you at odds with another leader without a valid reason, and if so, that you handle whatever the difference is in a godlike manner.

> ▶ Matthew 5:23–25, 18:15; Hebrews 12:14; 1 Timothy 5:17–21.

238. Make forgiveness and reconciliation a priority.

> ▶ Matthew 6:14–15; Luke 17:1–4;
> Mark 3:28–29; Ephesians 4:32; Colossians 3:13.

239. Never expose the members to people or fellowships that are ungodly. You may be strong enough to fellowship with a person or group that is out of order, but the lambs of your ministry may not be able to handle it.

> ▶ John 10:10–16; 2 Corinthians 6:14–18;
> 1 Corinthians 5:11; Proverbs 13:20;
> 1 Thessalonians 5:22; Exodus 34:12.

240. Don't allow any ungodly or rebellious spirit to approach your sacred desk (pulpit-podium). Beware of wolves in sheep's clothing: that spirit may have been sent to destroy your ministry.

> ▶ Matthew 7:6, 15, 10:16, 24:11; Acts 20:28–31.

241. Be careful who you receive advice from; everyone that you think is with you or for you may not be.

> ▶ 1 Kings 12:8–10; Numbers 31:16; 2 Chronicles 22:3;
> Job 2:9; Proverbs 13:10, 25:19.

242. Take heed to how you build; this includes your life, ministry, and your church.

> ▶ Psalm 119:9, 127; 1 Corinthians 3:9–17;
> Acts 20:32; Galatians 2:16–18.

243. Don't just teach tithing and giving, do it yourself as well.

> ▶ Malachi 3:10–11; Luke 6:38; Acts 4:33–35.

244. Never lord over God's inheritance. They are God's people and not yours.

> ▶ 1 Peter 5:2–3; Matthew 23:12; Obadiah 1:3–4.

245. Encourage the members to be at peace with one another. Don't manipulate them into hurting one another. Be a strong advocate of peace!

▶ Matthew 5:9; Hebrews 12:14; James 3:13–18.

246. Only go where God leads.

▶ Deuteronomy 32:11–12; Proverbs 20:24; Psalm 5:8, 119:133, 139:10, 143:10.

247. Take heed to the wisdom of wise and God-ordained elders, whether they are ministers or just mothers and fathers in the Gospel.

▶ 2 Chronicles 10:1–13; Job 12:12; Proverbs 12:15, 15:22; 1 Kings 12:6–13; 1 Timothy 5:17.

248. Give ear to the words of your godly and faithful members.

▶ Proverbs 8:33–34, 18:15.

249. Use caution and be prayerful about those you elevate, consecrate, put into positions, or sanction. "Lay hands suddenly on no man."

▶ 1 Timothy 5:21–25; 2 Timothy 1:6–7.

250. Do not publicly dishonor your associate leaders. Open rebuke or correction for sin is one thing, but humiliating people just because you can is not the will of God.

▶ Galatians 6:1; Proverbs 27:3–6; 1 Timothy 5:19–21; 2 Timothy 2:24–26; Jude 8–23.

251. Do not allow musicians, praise and worship leaders, choirs, or auxiliaries to hold your church hostage! Make sure your services start on time! Don't allow anyone to hinder the service of the Lord! Make sure God is in control and not people with gifts. Services should not be held up to wait for singers or musicians. Someone anointed should go forth and sing a cappella (without instrumental accompaniment) if they must! Who is in charge of your church, you or those with gifts?

▶ Romans 11:29; Ecclesiastes 3:1, 7:5; Proverbs 18:9; 1 Thessalonians 2:18.

Enhancing the Shepherd Leader/Overseer

252. If you have made a contract or agreement with a musician, etc., please take care of your obligation; but don't allow yourself or the church to be manipulated just for the sake of having music. Use integrity; keep your word.

▸ Proverbs 22:29; Jeremiah 22:13; James 5:4–12.

253. Avoid habitual lateness which is associated with unpreparedness and slothfulness. Be a good steward over time as an example for your members. You should be there for the opening of the service unless you have a reasonable explanation. There is no justifiable reason for you to make a grand entrance. This is not a show; you are to lead by example and not just by word only!

▸ Ecclesiastes 3:1, 17; Proverbs 18:9;
Matthew 25:1–13; 1 Peter 5:5–6; Acts 5:20–21a;
Hebrews 6:11–12; Romans 12:11.

254. Avoid embarrassing members over money. Gimmicks should not be used to coerce or shame them into giving. Make sure that you are teaching and exhorting them to give with sound doctrine based on true principles stated in the Word of God. Do not speak words that may cause you to be accused of being greedy, a lover of money, or labeled as a false prophet.

▸ Luke 6:38; 2 Peter 2:1–3; 2 Corinthians 9:6–7;
Deuteronomy 16:17; Matthew 6:1–4; Jeremiah 14:14.

255. Avoid disrupting worship services by arriving purposely late as if you are a celebrity. Jesus should be the main attraction of every worship service, and for sure, He beat you there! Don't take the focus off of Him and put it on yourself!

▸ Psalm 100:4; Isaiah 6:1–10, 8:13; 1 Peter 1:24–25, 5:8–9;
James 4:10, 17; Acts 12:21–23.

256. Seek the Lord for appropriate conflict management skills.

▸ James 1:5, 3:13–18; Psalm 71:1;
1 Kings 3:16–28, 4:29–30;
Proverbs 3:5–7; Isaiah 1:17–20.

257. Treat people from different denominations with respect. The true and living God will reveal Himself and true doctrine. Keep in mind Elijah's challenge to the prophets of Baal and the prayer to his God.

> ▶ 1 Kings 18:36–37; Matthew 12:30;
> Luke 6:44; 1 Thessalonians 5:12–13.

258. Always be ready to pray, preach, counsel, teach, and most of all witness concerning the Gospel of Jesus Christ.

> ▶ 1 Peter 3:15; 2 Timothy 4: 1–5.

259. Do not scatter God's people. Make sure that you are not responsible for anyone's departure from the ministry.

> ▶ Jeremiah 23:1–2; Ezekiel 34; Matthew 18:6–14.

260. Do not tolerate physical or spiritual bullying in your ministry in any form! Neither you nor auxiliary heads should bully God's people in any way in the church. Jesus is a gentleman and He invites us to make choices. He does not strong-arm or manipulate us even to accept Him. We should ask, request, or invite. Avoid putting unreasonable demands on His people. Remember, God sees and He knows all.

> ▶ Isaiah 32:5–6; Ecclesiastes 5:8; Ezekiel 22:29;
> Amos 5:12; Micah 7:2–4; Proverbs 15:3;
> Acts 26:11; 1 Peter 5:2–3.

261. Never allow anyone to leave the church offended without you as the leader trying to find out the reason for it. Pray about each situation and wait on God. Some people who depart do not wish to be sought after; whereas others may just need a little love and encouragement.

> ▶ James 3:1–18; Hebrews 12:12–14;
> Psalm 41:9, 55:12–14;
> Matthew 18:6–17; Ezekiel 34:1–6.

262. Take no responsibility, but pray for members who depart out of rebellion rather than by the leading of the Lord. If they are out of the will of God and have rejected righteous counseling, then they are going to need your love and prayers!

> ▶ Matthew 18:12–17; Jude 1:16–23; 1 John 2:19;
> 1 Timothy 4:1–2; 2 Timothy 4:10; Proverbs 21:16, 27:8.

263. Through prayer and discernment, use wisdom in receiving people for membership coming from other ministries. This is not a contest; don't receive people just to make other pastors or churches appear as though they are not good enough! Make sure that they have left that ministry properly. Consultations in some cases may be in order even for lay members. Copies of letters of resignation along with current credentials are always in order for associate leaders when applicable. Make sure that they left in good standing.

> ▶ 1 Thessalonians 5:12; Hebrews 5:14; 1 Corinthians 2:14.

264. Be prepared to comfort, encourage, and bind the wounded; and to correct and help heal those who are bitter coming from previous ministries. Some may be coming for refuge.

> ▶ Zechariah 13:6; Luke 4:18; Psalm 109:22, 147:3;
> Ephesians 4:31–32; Hebrews 12:14–15.

265. Be prepared for disappointment. There are times when members will leave without warning and without provocation, while others are absent because they struggle with being faithful. If they are not faithful to God, they will not be faithful to the church.

> ▶ 1 Timothy 4:1; Psalm 27:8, 119:176;
> Proverbs 21:16; John 6:66; Acts 13:13, 15:37–41.

266. Release, bless, and support those members who must depart from your ministry in obedience to the leading of the Lord. They and/or their works will always be an extension and a testament of your ministry. Be proud of them and encourage them according to the will of God.

> ▶ Genesis 12:1–4, 31:3; Deuteronomy 32:11–12;
> Acts 13:2–4; 2 Corinthians 3:5–14.

267. Never try to steal or coax another pastor's sheep (members) over to your church. Allow people to make their own choices by the leading of the Holy Spirit. Shepherds must always do what is in the best interest of the sheep according to the Will of God and not your ego. Beware however, of spiritual fugitives who may be running after they have sown seeds of discord in another ministry. Each one that comes to you for membership should receive consultation and/or correction if needed in the spirit of love.

> ▸ Exodus 20:15; Romans 2:21; 1 Peter 5:1–3.

268. Promote family or friends only according to sound doctrine and the leading of the Lord. Don't allow anyone to shipwreck your ministry!

> ▸ Micah 7:5–6; 2 Timothy 2:16–21; 1 Samuel 1:3, 2:12–34;
> 1 Chronicles 17:11–14; Proverbs 3:35;
> Psalm 75:5–7; 1 Samuel 3:13, 8:1–7.

269. Avoid the spirit of nepotism at all costs. Choose those whom God chooses as opposed to who is related to you. If God has chosen your relative, then so be it!

> ▸ 1 Chronicles 17:11–14, 22:7–13, 23:1, 26:10, 28:9–10;
> Psalm 75:5–7; Genesis 27:5–13; 1 Samuel 8:1–5.

270. Do not allow families or members in the church to control the ministry.

> ▸ Numbers 16:1–33; Judges 9:1–56; 1 Kings 11:4–11;
> 2 Chronicles 22:3; Micah 7:5–6; Matthew 14:8.

271. Do not allow other relationships or associations to control the ministry.

> ▸ Psalm 55:12–14, 56:1–6, 82:1–4; Micah 7:3–5;
> Exodus 34:12; Proverbs 24:1; Numbers 33:55–56;
> 1 Kings 11:2; 2 Corinthians 6:14–17; 2 Chronicles 19:2;
> 2 Thessalonians 3:6; Deuteronomy 16:18–19; Ephesians 5:11.

Enhancing the Shepherd Leader/Overseer

272. Again, be mindful of the people, but do not allow them to control you.

▶ 1 Samuel 15:17–24.

273. Consider doctrine and understand it, yet take heed through the Word of God and in respect to the organization to which you are a member.

▶ Proverbs 4:1–7; Hebrews 13:7–17; 1 Timothy 4:6–9; Titus 2.

274. Honor your commitment to an organization and its hierarchy according to godly doctrine and principles. Fearfully however, disassociate yourself and your ministry from doctrines of heresy.

▶ 1 Timothy 4, 6:1–6; Titus 3:9–10.

275. Honor your responsibility and allegiance to God.

▶ 2 Corinthians 4:5; Jeremiah 3:15; John 21:17; Matthew 15:8–9.

276. Remember that your inappropriate anger as a leader will get you into serious trouble with God!

▶ Numbers 20:7–12; Psalm 106:32–33; Ephesians 4:26–32; Ecclesiastes 7:9.

277. Know that you cannot be a good leader while disrespecting or neglecting your spouse or family. You should never use them as an excuse for not abiding in your calling. It is God's will however, that you nurture and provide for them.

▶ 1 Timothy 5:8; Proverbs 6:6–8, 12:7–11, 13:11; Esther 2:11; John 19:27; Genesis 30:30.

278. Remember that neither you nor your family will be blessed by disrespecting the people that God has assigned you to lead.

▶ 1 Timothy 3:11; 1 Samuel 2:22–25, 3:13, 8:1–4.

279. Despise not prophesying but rebuke spiritual fortune-telling.

> ▸ Ezekiel 13:1–3, Micah 3:11;
> Jeremiah 1:5, 2:8, 23:21–22, 28:9–15;
> 1 Corinthians 14:22–33; 1 John 4:1–6.

280. Count your blessings, but be careful in numbering God's people.

> ▸ 2 Samuel 24; 1 Chronicles 21:1–30.

281. Recognize the difference between one who is faithful and someone who has a take-over spirit.

> ▸ Luke 16:10–12; Psalm 101:6;
> 1 Corinthians 4:2–17; Romans 10:2.

282. Accept those God has sent to help you and utilize them.

> ▸ Exodus 4:10–30, 17:12; Judges 20:11;
> Nehemiah 4:16–17; Matthew 18:19;
> 2 Timothy 4:11; Romans 16:1–2.

283. Allow God to handle the Miriams, Sauls, and Absaloms in the house!

> ▸ Numbers 12; 1 Samuel 18:5–15; 2 Samuel 15:1–14.

284. Avoid jealousy and envy; look what it did to Saul.

> ▸ 1 Samuel 18:5–12; Song of Solomon 8:6;
> Acts 7:9–10; Luke 15:26–32.

285. Avoid profanity and perverse communication, even in your sermons.

> ▸ Proverbs 15:28, 18:21; Ecclesiastes 5:1–7;
> Matthew 26:71–75, 12:33–37; Ephesians 4:27–30;
> 2 Samuel 16:5–6, 17:42–43; Psalm 34:13; Exodus 20:7;
> Leviticus 19:12–14; James 3:10; Romans 3:13–18.

286. Take care of the Lord's house! Keep your service area and/or building clean, repaired, and looking presentable as much as possible. Never allow trash to be left behind or unsupervised children to run rampant in a manner that will destroy your place of worship. Is your own home in shambles and in need of repair? God shows concern about our places of worship and even our bodies as temples. How we care for both is a testament or an embarrassment to our commitment to Christ.

> ▶ Ecclesiastes 10:18; Haggai 1:3–14; Matthew 21:12–13;
> 1 Corinthians 3:16–17; Exodus 19:10–11.

287. Learn to know when the spirit of God is truly moving in your church, welcome Him and do not try to hinder or stop His work. Move with Him, and never get in His way! Make sure that it is His holy spirit in operation and not flesh on display.

> ▶ Isaiah 6:1–10, 64:1–2; 2 Corinthians 3:6–17;
> 1 Thessalonians 5:19; Ephesians 4:30.

288. Prayerfully identify the gifts and who has them in your ministry.

> ▶ Romans 12:3–8; 1 Corinthians 12:4–28, 14:1–32;
> Ephesians 4:7–19.

289. Allow the freedom of prayer, praise, worship, and prophecy to go forth in your ministry under the authority of the Holy Ghost. Through prayer, invoke and respect the "Cloud," or the "Shekinah" glory of God. When the Shekinah is present, no flesh will be able to stand in the presence of Almighty God! There are blessings such as deliverance and healing in the Cloud!

> ▶ 1 Timothy 2:8; John 4:23–24; Hebrews 2:12, 13:15;
> Acts 2:1–17; 2 Chronicles 5:11–14, 7:14;
> 1 Thessalonians 5:16–19; 2 Corinthians 3:17;
> Exodus 4:34–36; Isaiah 6:1–7.

290. Watch as well as pray. No matter where you are seated in the church stay in tune with the Holy Spirit enough to sense when something may be out of order. Also train your ushers, adjutants, or security persons to be vigilant and prayerful.

> ▶ Ezekiel 33:1–7; Matthew 26:40–41; Nehemiah 6:9–14;
> 2 Timothy 4:5; Psalm 84:10; 1 Corinthians 16:13; 1 Peter 5:8.

291. Lead firmly and faithfully, but affectionately.

> ▶ 2 Timothy 1:6–7, 13–14, 2:24–25.

292. Learn to care for and appreciate one member just as you would thousands.

> ▶ Judges 18:1–27; Luke 15:1–10; Matthew 5:1–2, 14:14–21.

293. Never open or close a ministry without clear direction and confirmation from God! The true church is God's people and not a building with four walls. Seek the Lord for His will and where you should hold services. You should never be ashamed to have service in a house or another type of building.

> ▶ Romans 8:14, 16:5; Galatians 5:16–17;
> Acts 16:6–13, 20:24; John 4:34, 17:4;
> 1 Corinthians 16:19; Philemon 1:2.

294. Remain faithful! Do not allow yourself to be intimidated by the lack of money or a lack of members. You must always walk by faith and not by sight.

> ▶ Matthew 10:7–14, 21:21–22; Ephesians 4:1–3;
> 2 Corinthians 5:7; Galatians 6:7–9; Judges 18:1–27.

295. Meditate and act upon the vision that God has ordained and not yours or anyone else's!

> ▶ Proverbs 4:26, 29:18; Acts 10:19–20, 26:19–32.

296. Pray for, and implement, revivals and fasting wisely. Revivals should not be used for fundraising or for featuring celebrity preachers but for the reviving and/or restoration of souls. Fasting is used to humble oneself as we petition God for help. It produces in us more of His spirit and less of us (flesh). It should never be used for evil as it was by Jezebel.

> ▶ Ezekiel 37:1–14; Hosea 14:4, 7; 1 Kings 21:9–19;
> Isaiah 57:15, 58; Psalm 138:7–8; Ezra 8:21–23;
> Jonah 3:5–10; Esther 4:16; Joel 2:28–32.

297. Wait to hear from God on any plans for your ministry.

> ▸ Proverbs 3:5–7; Habakkuk 2:1–4;
> Psalm 27:14, 37:23, 62:5; Hosea 12:6; Acts 16:4–10.

298. Learn to delegate authority and oversee that those who you have delegated do not usurp your authority and work evil.

> ▸ Genesis 27:35–36; Proverbs 25:19; 1 Peter 5:8;
> 2 Kings 5:20–27; 1 Samuel 13:7–14.

299. Know that there are responsibilities in the church that certain personality types cannot handle and that you should never assign to them. Trust the Holy Spirit!

> ▸ Acts 15:36–41, 13:13; Romans 16:17; Philippians 3:15–19;
> Hebrews 5:12; 1 Corinthians 3:12–16, 13:11, 14:20;
> 2 Timothy 2:20.

300. Be careful; all things should be done decent and in order, and carried out in the spirit of love. If a person you have assigned to a task cannot accomplish it with love then perhaps this is neither the job nor the season for them to have that authority.

> ▸ Proverbs 29:2; 1 Corinthians 14:40; Philippians 3:18–19;
> 2 Timothy 2:24; Ecclesiastes 3:1;
> 2 Thessalonians 1:3; Galatians 4:2.

301. Be an example of a kind, gentle, yet strong spiritual leader.

> ▸ 2 Timothy 1:6–14, 2:1–5; Philippians 1:9–21;
> James 3:17–18; Titus 3:1–4.

302. Make ministry your priority.

> ▸ Acts 6:4, 20:24; 1 Corinthians 4:1–2;
> Colossians 4:17; 2 Timothy 4:5.

303. Don't be a brawler. Don't make it difficult for people to approach you.

> ▸ 2 Timothy 2:24; Titus 3:2; Philippians 1:15;
> Proverbs 25:24–28, 26:21–27; Psalm 120:1–7.

304. Hold fast to the truth; don't be a sellout!

> ▸ Proverbs 23:23; John 8:32;
> Hebrews 4:14, 10:23; Revelation 3:3–11;

305. Wait with great expectation for God to fulfill His promises to you and the church.

> ▸ Psalm 62:5; Philippians 1:20; 2 Peter 3:8–9.

306. Learn to encourage yourself as well as the people.

> ▸ Judges 20:22; 1Samuel 30:6; Philippians 1:19–21.

307. Build relationships with others in ministry.

> ▸ Luke 8:21; Romans 16:1–16; Ephesians 2:19; James 5:17;
> Proverbs 18:24; John 10:16, 15:14; Acts 18:7.

308. Don't give up on your own dreams; trust in the Lord to bring them to fruition as well. Seek the Lord about how to accomplish those goals while you are serving Him. He cares about those dreams just as much as you do.

> ▸ Psalm 37:3–7, 84:11, 145:15–19;
> Proverbs 10:24; Jeremiah 29:11–13.

309. Always remember that though you are an instrument of God, you are yet still human.

> ▸ Psalm 103:14; Romans 7:15–21; 1 Corinthians 1:26–29;
> 2 Corinthians 10:3–7; 2 Corinthians 12:1–10.

310. Weep if you must; tears of travail sown in private will yield tears of joy in public!

> ▸ Psalm 6:6, 30:5, 34:15–22, 56:8, 126:5; Matthew 6:4–18;
> Acts 20:19; 2 Timothy 1:1–4; Job 16:20.

311. Never use the sacred desk/pulpit for brawling and disorderly conduct! Who will ever feel the love of Jesus from that polluted place again? Do not use consecrated, holy places or objects for purposes other than that which is holy. The apostles avoided profaning the holy things, do you?

> ▸ Acts 24:6–21; Zephaniah 3:4; Ecclesiastes 5:1–2;
> Psalm 89:7; Joshua 5:15; Proverbs 25:28.

312. Watch your step: "Keep thy foot when thou goest into the house of the Lord."

> ▸ Ecclesiastes 5:1–8; Leviticus 19:30;
> Psalm 89:7; Habakkuk 2:20; John 2:16.

313. Always operate in a spirit of integrity.

> Proverbs 20:7; Job 2:3, 27:1–6; 2 Corinthians 7:1–2;
> 2 Peter 3:14; Romans 13; 1 Samuel 12:1–5.

314. Encourage your members to continue in love for the sinner, the backslider and those that leave the ministry who may cast your name and the church's out as evil.

> ▸ John 3:16–17; Matthew 5:11–12, 5:43–48, 18:21–22;
> Galatians 6:1–10.

315. Allow your life and the service you give to be the best sermon that you could ever preach. You may not think that you preach as well as someone else, but leading by example makes for a better sermon.

> ▸ 1 Timothy 4:12, 5:17; 2 Thessalonians 3:9;
> Galatians 5:1; Titus 2:7.

316. Be a vessel of honor and not one to dishonor. Live above reproach.

> ▸ 2 Timothy 2:20–21; 1 Thessalonians 4:4; 2 Peter 3:14.

317. Humble yourself and avoid this spirit of arrogance that has crept into the church. Don't allow yourself to become haughty, high-minded and full of pride, thinking yourself to be better than others just because of your ministry. Warn, rebuke, and counsel in the spirit of love those in your ministry who behave in this manner. Help them to understand the importance of a spirit of humility.

> ▸ Proverbs 8:13, 21:4, 26:12, 27:1–2;
> Romans 12:3, 12:16; Isaiah 13:11; 1 Corinthians 8:2.

318. Remember to watch as well as pray.

> ▸ Matthew 25:13; Luke 12:37;
> 1 Thessalonians 5:6–14; 1 Peter 5:8.

319. Never allow anyone to disrespect God's house and/or to disrupt the service of worship. Rebuke any spirit that seeks to cause disturbances (tumults) in the church especially during worship service. Teach your ushers and security personnel to be watchful for breaches of security and for spiritual warfare that will disturb the divine order of God!

> ▸ 1 Corinthians 14:33; James 3:16;
> Acts 13:6–12, 21:34; Leviticus 19:30.

320. The disrespect of cell phone use during worship service is the enemy's way of using us to dishonor God. Have not cell phones become idols? Whether service is being held in a church, a hall, a house or down by the river, it is a sacred event and we should respect it as such. As leaders, we must be the example and the teacher that will persuade God's people not to fall into this trap!

> ▸ Exodus 3:5; Leviticus 19:30; Ecclesiastes 5:1;
> Psalm 89:7; John 2:16; Hebrews 12:27–29.

321. We have the responsibility to teach our members and their children to respect prayer, praise, and worship. Refrain from excessive talking and revelry. You cannot expect them to respect you if you do not respect the things of God.

> ▸ 1 Thessalonians 5:19; Hebrews 1:6–7; Deuteronomy 6:7;
> Ecclesiastes 5:1, 12; Leviticus 19:30; Proverbs 22:6;
> Luke 11:1; Ephesians 6:4; John 2:16; Matthew 21:15.

322. Members who do not engage in active prayer time should not be allowed to serve on any auxiliary in the church. Unwillingness to pray will be the defeat, and the demise of the church and the assignment He has given you. Prayer is communication with God; so therefore how can anyone serve someone they don't talk to?

> ▶ 1 Timothy 2:8; 1 John 5:14–15; James 4:17;
> Luke 18:1; Matthew 6:4–13, 26:41; 1 Chronicles 16:11;
> 1 Thessalonians 5:17; Jeremiah 29:13.

323. Do not be afraid to release rebellious leaders from positions until they have had time to repent and humble themselves. Follow the leading of the Lord.

> ▶ 1 Timothy 4:1–2, 5:17–21; Titus 1:10–16, 2:15;
> 1 Samuel 15:19–35; 2 Thessalonians 3:14–15.

324. Always be prepared to humble yourself if you are at fault. Be willing to apologize to your family, church, friends, and even your employer if necessary.

> ▶ Numbers 22:14; Joshua 7:20; 2 Samuel 24:10;
> Proverbs 16:18–19; James 4:6–10; 1 Peter 5:5–6;
> Matthew 5:20–26; Luke 15:17–19; Psalm 28:13.

325. Leave no room for the devil. Leave nothing for him to spot your life.

> ▶ Ephesians 4:23–27; 2 Peter 3:14.

326. A word of wisdom from a wise pastor: "You are not responsible for how someone treats you, but for how you treat them." (Satchell 1975–1999)

> ▶ Matthew 12:36–37; Romans 14:12.

327. Give time and attention to every age group in your congregation.

> ▶ Proverbs 16:31, 22:6; Psalm 71:17–18;
> 1 Timothy 4:12; Matthew 19:14;
> Leviticus 19:32; Ecclesiastes 12:1–7.

328. Always consider the spiritual welfare of God's people.

> ▸ Isaiah 35:3–4; 2 Corinthians 12:10–21;
> 1 Thessalonians 3:10; 2 Samuel 24:17–25;
> Ezekiel 34:1–6.

329. Love God with all of your heart, mind, body, and soul.

> ▸ Deuteronomy 6:5; Jeremiah 29:11–14;
> 1 Chronicles 22:18–19.

330. Set the house in order. Do this by the leading of the Lord when necessary.

> ▸ Titus 1:5; 1 Corinthians 6:1–8, 11:34, 14:23, 33–40;
> Colossians 2:5.

331. Preach the Word, whether you are preaching to one or one thousand!

> ▸ Acts 5:42, 8:26–40; Isaiah 40:8; Hebrews 4:12;
> Matthew 4:4; Psalm 68:11, 107:20; Isaiah 50:4–7;
> 1 Corinthians 1:21, 9:16; 2 Timothy 4:2; John 1:1.

332. Do not make up sermons on your own or copy from others. Spend quality time in the presence of God in prayer so that you can receive a word from Him for His people.

> ▸ Jeremiah 30:1–2; Matthew 8:8, 10:27;
> 2 Timothy 2:15; Psalm 119:11, 140:13, 147:19;
> Proverbs 15:23; 2 Thessalonians 2:17; Hebrews 5:13;
> Jeremiah 23:29–31; Colossians 3:16; Isaiah 28:9–10.

333. Meditate on God's Word daily.

> ▸ Psalm 119:15–16, 48, 78, 148.

334. Ask God for wisdom.

> ▸ Proverbs 4:7–13, 16:16, 23:4; 2 Chronicles 1:10–13;
> Ecclesiastes 7:19, 9:16–18; James 1:5–8;
> Colossians 1:9–11; Ephesians 1:17.

335. Don't be afraid of failure.

> ▶ Isaiah 41:10–13; Hebrews 13:6; Psalm 112:5–8;
> 2 Timothy 1:7; James 1:1–3.

336. Yes, sometime you will feel rejected!

> ▶ 2 Chronicles 36:16; Luke 7:30, 10:16;
> Galatians 4:16; Mark 6:3; John 1:11, 12:48.

337. You may get tired sometimes; but do not be weary.

> ▶ Galatians 6:9; 2 Thessalonians 3:13–16;
> 2 Corinthians 4:1, 4:16; Revelation 2:3.

338. Always remember: other leaders have survived and so will you!

> ▶ 1 Peter 2:19–23, 4:1, 5:6–10; Hebrews 6:10–15;
> 2 Corinthians 12:9–15; 1 Corinthians 4:9–14;
> 2 Chronicles 30:10, 36:16; Acts 14:19–20.

339. Remember that God is on your side!

> ▶ Psalm 118:6, 124:1–8.

340. Don't allow your flesh (your old self) to take control. Keep walking in the Spirit.

> ▶ Romans 6:2–14, 8:5–14, 8:36–39, 12:1–3;
> Colossians 3:3–17; 2 Corinthians 5:17.

341. Deny yourself.

> ▶ Matthew 16:24–26; Mark 8:34–38; Luke 18:29–30;
> Romans 15:1; Philippians 3:8–11.

342. Utilize your finances and the church's wisely.

> ▶ 1 Chronicles 9:26; Nehemiah 5:1–13, 10:37–39;
> Genesis 47:15–28; 2 Corinthians 7:2; Mark 10:19;
> Romans 13:6–8; 1 Corinthians 6:8–10; Acts 4:32–37.

343. Don't lose your focus!

> ▶ Psalm 119:37, 121:1–2; Proverbs 4:25;
> Matthew 4:8, 6:33, 14:23–31; Joshua 7:21.

344. Learn to take time off and rest. Do it for the church as well as yourself. Try to rest also after you have ministered and prayed for people. You need refreshing after this.

> ▶ Genesis 2:2; 1 Corinthians 16:18; Exodus 34:21;
> Leviticus 23:3; Psalm 3:5, 4:8, 127:1–2;
> Jeremiah 31:26; Mark 4:38, 6:30–32; 1 Kings 19:5.

345. Make it a point to spend quality time with your family and friends.

> ▶ Genesis 46:29–30, 47:12.

346. Learn to laugh and enjoy the life and the call God has ordained for you.

> ▶ Ecclesiastes 3:1–4; Psalm 30:1–5, Psalm 126; Proverbs 17:22.

347. Do not be intimidated by customs and traditions of men.

> ▶ Colossians 2:8; Titus 1:14; Colossians 2:20–23.

348. Ask yourself: "Why should I be afraid of the people whom God has called me to serve?"

> ▶ Matthew 10:28; Mark 4:40; Luke 12:2–7; 1 Samuel 15:24;
> Jeremiah 1:4–10; Isaiah 50:7; 2 Timothy 1:7.

349. Never seek to undermine the Lord, your organization, or the overseer. And whatever your role in it is, be sure to glorify God by fulfilling it.

> ▶ Colossians 3:12–25, 4:17.

350. Just a reminder: all vices should be avoided! Addictions such as smoking, drinking, drugs, sex, and gambling will ruin your witness and ultimately cause you to lose in the end! If you are engaging in these activities, it is because you have not yet been delivered from a nature of carnality. You may have been called, *but you are not clean*; so your true purpose is being thwarted by your flesh, consequently giving the enemy control over you and ministry. Diligently seek deliverance from this type of bondage. Humbling yourself and admitting you have a problem would be one of the first steps toward your victory.

> ▶ Romans 6:23, 11:29; Psalm 34:18;
> 1 John 1:8–10; 2 Corinthians 7:9–11;
> Galatians 5:19–21; Ephesians 4:17–30, 5:1–10;
> Jude 1:1–25.

351. BE WARNED! Your spouse, family, friends, adjutants, deacons, elders, missionaries, evangelists, security personnel, ushers, and members should be an extension and a manifestation of your leadership of excellence. Leaders have the potential to reproduce other leaders. If you are a corrupt leader, then you will produce other corrupt leaders such as yourself. God's people are not to serve as your personal, physical, or spiritual gang members, hit men, henchmen, or enforcers! Each one of them, regardless of their title is a disciple of Jesus Christ; and they deserve better than that from you. Always exercise wisdom as you remain approachable and accessible to God's people without showing partiality. Rebuke and counsel those who behave rashly and/or arrogantly.

> ▶ Matthew 7:15–20, 23:1–28; 1 Timothy 4:12;
> 1 Kings 21:7–15, 25; John 18:10–11; Luke 9:50–56;
> 2 Kings 5:20–27; Titus 2:7–8; 1 Chronicles 23:28.

Sack Four
REFINING THE EVANGELIST/MISSIONARY

352. Decide whether missionary work or evangelism is really your calling. Are you willing to accept it at any cost?

> ▶ Isaiah 6:7–12; Matthew 28:19–20;
> Mark 16:15–18; Luke 10:1–12; Acts 5:42, 21:8, 22:21;
> 1 Peter 3:15; Ephesians 4:11.

353. Do you expect to charge for your service rather than receive a freewill offering? Do you belong to a ministry that is willing to support this type of ministry? Are you willing to trust God to provide for you in the area of finances?

> ▶ 2 Kings 5:26; Luke 10:2–8; Mark 16:15–20;
> 1 Corinthians 9:1–18, 10:23–26; 2 Corinthians 11:7–14.

354. As you abide in your calling, sacrifices are sometimes necessary; yet use caution with those who may try to take advantage of your ministry or gift. Get a clear understanding of your travel arrangements and the finances involved ahead of time. If you encounter this scenario, remember to pray for those responsible. Consult the Lord and discuss things such as this with your leader.

> ▶ Matthew 10:7–10; Acts 8:18–24; 2 Corinthians 11:7–12.

355. Can you handle an assignment in missions, especially in the foreign field? Cultures, climates, and governing rules are different. Are you prepared? Certain credentials, such as a passport and visa, are necessary (make sure they are updated and current).

> ▶ Matthew 28:19–20; Mark 13:10, 16:15–18;
> Acts 1:8; Acts 22:21; 1 Corinthians 9:18–23.

356. Before you go through that open door to accept a preaching engagement, be sure that it was God who opened it. Did God release you, or are you going on your own?

> ▶ 1 Corinthians 16:9; Matthew 2:12; Acts 16:6–10;
> 2 Corinthians 2:10–12; Colossians 4:2–3.

357. Never go out to minister anywhere without proper apostolic release. It is wise to have the approval and sanctioning of your leader. Respect your spiritual covering.

> ▶ Jeremiah 14:14, 23:21; John 20:21;
> 1 Timothy 4:14; Acts 5:19–20, 13:1–5.

358. Before you go to minister, fast, pray, study and rest in preparation for possible spiritual warfare that may await you.

> ▶ Genesis 2:2; 1 Corinthians 16:9, 15–18;
> Acts 6:4, 13:2–12; Psalm 4:8; Proverbs 3:24;
> Joshua 1:8; 1 Kings 19:4–7; Jeremiah 3:26;
> 1 Thessalonians 3:10; Colossians 4:2–3.

359. Plan and confirm your travel arrangements including dates, addresses, phone numbers, and the person responsible (the hosting pastor or representative) for your expenses ahead of time. Allow the Lord to guide you. Always handle your business with integrity.

> ▶ 1 Corinthians 16:4–18; Acts 16:7–13; Judges 18:1–20
> Proverbs 22:29; Philemon 1:20–22; Ephesians 6:20–22;
> Titus 3:12–15; Matthew 2:12; Ecclesiastes 3:1.

360. *Confirm the assignment* with the hosting pastor so you do not end up in an embarrassing situation. Never, ever assume anything; make sure that you have a clear understanding of your purpose for being there. Examples: Are you the primary preacher, or one of many? Are you invited there to preach, pray, sing, or what? Are you to receive an offering or are you expected to bring one?

> ▸ Proverbs 17:27, 22:29; Romans 15:22–28;
> 1 Timothy 1:3; Philippians 4:14–19;
> Acts 20:1–22, 28:23a; 1 Corinthians 16:10–18.

361. If you continue receiving a check in your spirit or have serious reservations about an engagement, it is ok to cancel! Be obedient to the Holy Spirit; don't just go to save face.

> ▸ Acts 16:6–13; Romans 8:14; John 16:13; Matthew 2:12.

362. Individuals who are married or are single parents of young children should ensure that their home/house/family is in proper order prior to departure. Don't bring shame and reproach on your ministry by not taking care of your family.

> ▸ 1 Timothy 5:8; Genesis 30:30; Romans 12:11;
> Hebrews 13:4; Ecclesiastes 9:9; 1 Corinthians 7:33.

363. Always dress appropriately for ministry, by adorning yourself as a holy vessel of God. Test your garment! If it will not endure the postures of worship, prayer and praise, the stains of blood, sweat and tears, a grip of anguish or a comforting embrace, then it is inappropriate! Our outward appearance should reflect our inward commitment and public witness of Christ and our personal regard for His people. If what you are wearing hinders ministry, then it is absolutely unacceptable!

> ▸ Genesis 35: 2; 1 Corinthians 1:8–9; 1 Thessalonians 4:4;
> Psalm 6:6, 95:6, 119:143; Isaiah 23:9, 45:23; Job 16:20;
> Luke 22:41–44; Acts 20:10; Hebrews 12:1; Exodus 28:2–4.

Refining the Evangelist/Missionary

364. When traveling out of town or out of the country, be prepared for differences in customs, culture, as well as climate and how it affects their mode of travel and worship. Services are held in camps, tents, huts, houses, as well as open air. Be prepared to humble yourself and endure.

> ▶ Acts 16:7–13, 20–21; 2 Timothy 2:3.

365. Use wisdom when traveling, either take extra cash or a legitimate credit card with you in the event of unexpected emergencies. This is modern-day ministry; we must couple wisdom with our faith. Make sure that you can always get back home! Be guided by the Holy Spirit.

> ▶ Proverbs 10:3–5; Matthew 10:16; Psalm 91:1–6;
> Romans 13:6–8; 1 Peter 5:8; James 4:13–17;
> Philippians 4:10–19; 1 Thessalonians 4:11–12.

366. Commit to being a blessing to God's people and not a physical (making unnecessary demands) or financial (expecting unreasonable amounts of money) burden.

> ▶ 2 Corinthians 2:4, 11:28, 12:11–16a;
> 1 Corinthians 9:22, 10:33; 1 Thessalonians 2:3–12;
> Romans 1:11; Acts 20:28.

367. Avoid becoming loud and unruly over money. If you are not blessed financially in one place, know that God will bless you in some other way. He can cause the blessings to come from another source.

> ▶ Matthew 5:44; Philippians 4:10–19; 1 Timothy 6:10.

368. Regardless of your title, once you arrive at your destination you are under that pastor's authority. Please give him/her the utmost respect as you would your own leader.

> ▶ Hebrews 13:17; 1 Peter 5:1–6.

369. Familiarize yourself with the doctrinal teachings of your destination ministry. Don't end up embarrassed because you preached something with which they were not in agreement. However, be led by the Holy Spirit; because what He tells you to preach may be what they need to hear, even if it means they may never invite you back again.

> ▶ Colossians 2: 6–9; Hebrews 13:9.

370. Remain a person of integrity even amid extreme pressure and persecution.

> ▶ Matthew 5:20; 2 Corinthians 12:9–10; Proverbs 11:3;
> Proverbs 20:7; 1 Peter 2:2–25; James 4:6–11.

371. Remember to depart and arrive with the proper, godly attitude. You are a visiting preacher and not the pastor. Don't usurp authority from that pastor; they will have to deal with that congregation once your assignment is over.

> ▶ 1 Thessalonians 2:9–10; 1 Timothy 3:15;
> 1 Samuel 18:5; Philippians 2:15.

372. Expect miracles to take place!

> ▶ 1 Corinthians 12:6–11; Psalm 62:5; Mark 16:17–18;
> Acts 8:6, 20:9–12, 14:3.

373. Arrive at your destination as a minister of peace and hopefully leave the same way—unless the gospel is rejected thereby causing you to have to "shake the dust from your feet."

> ▶ Matthew 10:14; Mark 6:10–11; Luke 9:5; Acts 13:50–52.

374. Don't give out your hotel location and/or room number to congregants while you are there to minister.

> ▶ Proverbs 2:11, 22:3; Isaiah 28:26; John 8:59, 11:59;
> 1 Corinthians 6:3; 1 Thessalonians 5:22.

375. Personal visiting from house to house is not a wise thing to do when you visit a city to do a crusade or revival in a large facility; this is a seedbed for disaster! House-to-house visiting would only apply in cases where churches are literally in the homes. Recreational visiting should be cautiously limited to after the crusade is over or upon the completion of your assignment.

> ▶ Matthew 10:12–15; 2 Timothy 3:5–7.

376. No matter how you are treated as a man or woman of God, always be pleasant and show kindness, as you operate in a spirit of excellence and integrity—and not with a snobbish or condescending attitude.

> ▶ Matthew 5:44–48, Proverbs 2:5–21.

377. Take care of yourself; rest, eat properly, follow your medication regimen (if applicable) while you are waiting for full healing to manifest. Also exercise, drink plenty of water, and change your wet or soiled clothing after ministering each and every time.

> ▶ 1 Kings 19:4–7; Psalm 91; Exodus 15:26; 2 Timothy 4:20;
> 1 Timothy 5:23 (Advised as a substitute remedy for poor water conditions.) Philippians 2:27–30; Acts 27:33–35.

378. Upon arriving at your hotel or other dwelling place, pray and prepare for the task ahead of you. Avoid excessive talking, even with the leader, because you want to be led by the Holy Ghost as to what you should say to God's people. Please do not allow yourself to be used to carry out a pastor's or a member's dirty work. Don't even listen to your own flesh! Preach only what God tells you to speak!

> ▶ Isaiah 29:15; James 1:26; Psalm 39:1, 55:12–14;
> Ecclesiastes 5:1–7; Ephesians 6:12; Proverbs 21:23.

379. Remember, you are on a spiritual assignment only! Your task does not include personal networking, friendships, or giving your opinions to members of that church. This behavior can literally strangle your ministry and shut you down. Know that it was not the devil; it was Y-O-U!

> ▸ Ephesians 4:1–4, 5:15–17, 6:12;
> 1 Thessalonians 2:10; Proverbs 6:12–14.

380. Avoid fellowshipping with people until after your assignment is completed, if possible. Stay consecrated!

> ▸ Proverbs 4:23–27; Titus 3:8; 2 Timothy 4:1–5;
> John 9:4; Ephesians 5:11.

381. Upon your arrival to the church or convention center, never, and we do mean never, invade the office space of that leader without their prior permission!

> ▸ 1 Timothy 5:17; Romans 12:10, 13:7–9;
> 1 Corinthians 14:40; Luke 14:8–11; Proverbs 25:6–7.

382. Do your best to always be on time for ministry; be diligent. Don't leave a pastor and their congregation waiting.

> ▸ Matthew 25:8–13; 1 Peter 3:8;
> Proverbs 10:4, 12:24, 22:29; Ecclesiastes 3:1.

383. Always wait for the arrival of the leader before you enter the pulpit. If the leader left other instructions, then follow the protocol as directed.

> ▸ 1 Timothy 5:17; Luke 14:8–11; Proverbs 25:6–7.

384. Preach the Word God gave you even when the congregation seems unresponsive or does not appear to be receptive. People respond differently in different cultures; do your best to please God.

> ▸ 2 Timothy 4:1–5; Matthew 13:3–9.

385. Keep your ear at God's mouth and obey His commands.

> ▸ 1 John 3:24; Hebrews 2:1; Proverbs 8:33–34;
> James 1:19; Mark 4:24; Psalm 94:8–11.

386. Your prophetic gift should be in operation during your ministering at the church service and not from your hotel room or by loud displays in public areas.

> ▶ Psalm 101:2; Philippians 1:10;
> Matthew 6:1–6, 23:5; 1 Corinthians 14:1–32.

387. If you were not invited to counsel the members of that church, then study to be quiet and allow the shepherd of that flock to do it.

> ▶ 1 Thessalonians 4:11; Ecclesiastes 5:2; 1 Corinthians 14:33.

388. If God has not given you a word for His people, then study to be quiet by holding your peace and waiting on Him! God gets no glory nor are the people edified when you operate in your flesh and try to make up something to say.

> ▶ Hebrews 5:12–15; Ecclesiastes 5:1–7;
> Jeremiah 14:14, 23:16–32, 28:15;
> Deuteronomy 18:20–22.

389. Don't be a spiritual fortune-teller. If you have the gift of prophecy, let it be under the direction of the Holy Ghost. Make sure of the authorship and authenticity. If God has not truly sent that Word, then refrain from speaking lies! Avoid public proclamations regarding worldly/material things such as matchmaking, wealth, and elevations. Know that if you speak anything attributing it to God, and it is not so, then you will have to answer for it on the Day of Judgment!

> ▶ Jeremiah 2:8, 5:31, 23:16–32, 28:9; Matthew 7:15; Mark 13:22;
> Deuteronomy 18:20–22; Hosea 9:7–8; Ezekiel 13:2–8.

390. Don't leave a mess for the pastor to have to clean up after you are gone!

> ▶ Jeremiah 23:1–18; 1 Corinthians 14:32–33;
> Titus 1:16, 3:8; Matthew 24:11.

Sack Five
CLARIFYING THE RESPONSIBILITIES OF AN APPOINTMENT

(Appointees: associate/ interim pastors, deacons, board members, trustees, officers, administrative personnel)

391. Now that you have received this appointment, examine yourself "Am I saved and sanctified? Have I been delivered? Am I filled with the Holy Ghost? Just because a leader appointed you does not confirm your salvation or your deliverance. If your answer is "no" to any of these questions, then explain to him/her that you need to work on your own soul's salvation first before accepting the position. Accepting a position in the work of the Lord with a carnal mind will only increase the pride of a sinner and strengthen the belief that his works will save him. Until then, there is no need to go any further in this book if you cannot answer the questions with an honest "yes!"

> ▶ John 3:16–17, 17:17–19; Acts 2:4, 6:1–3, 11:24, 13:1–5;
> 1 Timothy 3:6–13; 2 Corinthians 13:5; Romans 8:1–8;
> 1 Thessalonians 5:23; Ephesians 2:8–9; Luke 1:15.

392. Make sure you filled with the Holy Ghost? It is an advised requirement. Although you were appointed, having the experience of the indwelling of the Holy Spirit will help you to work more honestly and effectively in the service of the Lord.

> ▶ John 14:26, 15:26, 16:7–15;
> Acts 1:8, 6:1–15, 7:55–60; 1 Timothy 3:6–13.

393. The assumption here is that if you were appointed, then you most certainly must be under a covering. By all means, respect and honor the church or religious organization where you have received this appointment. Should you leave that ministry, don't assume that the next leader or overseer has to appoint you to the same position. They are not familiar with your walk with Christ or your experience in church work.

> ▶ 1 Thessalonians 5:12–13; Ephesians 4:1–2;
> Proverbs 25:14; 1 Corinthians 9:19; 1 Peter 2:12–13;
> 2 Timothy, 3:1–7, 4:5, 1 Timothy 5:17–25.

394. Please make sure that you have the proper credentials or approval for the office for which you have been appointed if needed. If you have come from another ministry, never, ever, lie about positions you have held in that ministry!

> ▶ Galatians 6:4; Proverbs 25:14;
> Titus 3:1–8; 1 Thessalonians 5:21.

395. Evaluate the reasons why you have received this appointment. Have you been appointed because of your family or friend affiliation? Do you believe that the one who appointed you was led by the Lord, or perhaps because there was no one else to fill the position, or because you were the next in line? Consider the responsibility and honor of the appointment.

> ▶ Exodus 4:14–17; Numbers 4:19, 11:14–17, 27:15–23;
> 1 Kings 11:18b; 1 Samuel 21:2; Proverbs 25:6–10;
> Matthew 20:21–22.

396. Do you believe in prayer, or do you just leave it for the leader and prayer warriors to do? How is your own individual prayer life? Because you are a part of the support system for the church, you should always have a prayer life.

> ▶ 1 Chronicles 16:11; Daniel 6:10; Luke 18:1;
> Matthew 26:41; Psalm 55:16–17;
> Ephesians 6:18; 1 Thessalonians 5:17.

397. Bow down and count up the cost! An attitude of humility is crucial for those in the "ministry of helps."

> ▶ Luke 10:1–20, 14:25–33; 1 Kings 19:20;
> Phillipians 2:7; 1 Corinthians 12:28–31.

398. Do you have a heart for "kingdom building" for the Lord, or for making a name for yourself? Take heed to how you build!

> ▶ 1 Corinthians 3:10–15; Ephesians 2:18–22;
> 1 Peter 2:5; Phillipians 2:7.

399. Always remember that you too are responsible for bringing in and ministering to souls. Sheep beget sheep, meaning "birth." What? Is this ministry where you serve not good enough to share with your family and friends? If your answer is "no," then why are you there?

> ▶ John 1:41–45, 5:43; Proverbs 11:30; Matthew 9:37–38;
> Acts 16:15, 33; 1 Corinthians 1:16, 4:14–16;
> Romans 16:6–16; 1 Timothy 5:4.

400. Please understand that some of you have been appointed to assist with the business of the church to free your leader up so he or she can concentrate on the Word—not so you can usurp authority from them.

> ▶ Acts 6:1–7; 2 Chronicles 28:14–15;
> 1 Corinthians 10:24, 16:15–16;
> Matthew 25:35–45; 2 Kings 5:15–27.

Clarifying the Responsibilities of an Appointment

401. Can you handle working behind the scenes and perhaps receiving little or no recognition?

> ▸ Luke 6:35; Matthew 10:42;
> 1 Corinthians 15:58, 16:10–11, 16:15–16.

402. Is your spouse in agreement with this appointment; are they willing to accept your responsibility and commitment to it?

> ▸ Luke 14:20; Proverbs 19:13–14, 31:10–12;
> Amos 3:3; 1 Timothy 3:8–16.

403. Please remember that your appointment means "working in the ministry for the body of Christ." This is not an opportunity to satisfy your personal needs or whims. Sacrifices must be made.

> ▸ Hebrews 13:16; John 9:4; 1 Corinthians 3:1–15.

404. Do you have the spirit of a manipulator? Repent! Are you with your ministry to work or to tear it down?

> ▸ 1 Kings 21:1–15; Mark 14:11;
> Matthew 26:47–50; Acts 19:24–32.

405. Get an understanding from the beginning; does the church where you attend belong to you or to the Lord? Is the church owned by an organization, a founder, board members, deacons, family members, or a community? Make everyone aware of it from the beginning so that there's no confusion as to who is in control. If you have no authority, then do not play the role.

> ▸ Proverbs 4:5–9, 14:6; 1 Thessalonians 4:6; Colossians 3:9.

406. You must be willing to humble yourself and take direction from the Lord through the leadership of your pastor.

> ▸ Hebrews 13:7, 17; Luke 22:24–27; Matthew 18:4;
> Romans 12:3; 1 Peter 5:5–9.

407. Ask yourself whether you are investing your service, time, or money as a way to secure control or power over the ministry or its leader?

▸ Acts 8:18–21; Matthew 23:28; 1 Timothy 6:16–19.

408. Make sure that you are familiar with the doctrine of your ministry and that you are in agreement with it and are willing to teach it to others. How can you hold positions in a ministry to which you are not committed?

▸ 1 Timothy 4:16–17; Hebrews 13:7–9; Colossians 2:6–8.

409. Do you really think that your money is the answer to all things? Do you try to manipulate God and the church with your money? Will you commit bribery as well as take bribes? Be careful how you give it out and how you receive it.

▸ Psalm 116:12–14; Matthew 22:15–22; Joel 2:12–13; Acts 8:18–20; Esther 3:8–10; Luke 18:12.

410. Remember; neither the Lord nor the church is a prostitute! He is the bridegroom, she is the bride; your money will not cause Him or the church to accept your deeds and give you what you want. Your money is not to be sent to the church in place of your presence and righteous living! You cannot buy yourself a seat in the Kingdom and thus there are no seats for sale in the church!

▸ Deuteronomy 16:18–19; Psalm 116:12–14; Matthew 20:20–28, 23:18–28; Joel 2:12–13; Hebrews 10:25; Romans 14:17.

411. Be mindful of the rules governing your position as well as the church.

▸ Hebrews 13:7, 17; 1 Corinthians 7:17; 1 Timothy 3:1–13.

Clarifying the Responsibilities of an Appointment

412. Upon accepting an appointment, understand that God works in seasons, and He can determine when that season is over. If and when your time is up, learn to humbly and graciously bow out, making room for the next person He has chosen.

▶ Proverbs 4:7, 17:27–28, 24:3; Ecclesiastes 3:1, 17.

413. Board members should be aware that though you may be a part of the infrastructure of the local church, the true spiritual foundation of the church is Jesus Christ.

▶ 1 Corinthians 3:11–15; Isaiah 28:16; Matthew 21:42; Ephesians 2:20–22.

414. Never be misguided in your thinking by having the notion that the church cannot function without you; God will always provide himself a "ram in the bush."

▶ Proverbs 3:5–6; 1 Samuel 14:6, 15:18–28; 1 Kings 19:14–18; Genesis 22:7–14.

415. Just because you were appointed to your position and are operating as second in command does not mean that you aren't responsible to pray and fast along with the ministry. You are to follow the example of righteousness of your leader.

▶ Matthew 26:40–46; 1 Thessalonians 5:17, 25; 1 Timothy 4:12; Acts 6:4.

416. Be ready to preach, teach, and exhort as you are instructed. Be sure to study the Word and be prepared for all situations.

▶ 1 Timothy 3:2–13; 2 Timothy 2:14–16, 3:16–17.

417. Appointed leaders also have a responsibility to the sick and shut-in. They should see to those who are widowed, incarcerated, grief stricken, and those who are in need. Hospital visitation should be brief, polite and effective. Talk faith and not doubt; speak life not death; consider the feelings of the family. Absolutely no loud noise is appropriate at any time.

▶ 2 Kings 8:4–6; Matthew 25:35–36; James 5:13–15; Acts 6:1–3.

418. Those that hold these offices should also be prepared for the many facets of service within the church such as overseeing and stocking educational materials, supplies for communion, offering, general maintenance, etc. or wherever they can serve. They too should know how to conduct the different services that are carried out in the church.

> ▸ Mark 8:1–9, 14:12–17; Matthew 26:17–19;
> 1 Chronicles 9:23–32, 15:23, 23:28.

419. Be careful how you conduct your meetings. Do not take on the spirit of a dictator. All business should be conducted in excellence but administrated in love.

> ▸ Romans 12:9–11, 13:10; Proverbs 22:29;
> 1 Thessalonians 5:12–15.

420. Profanity is always unacceptable as it reveals your denial of Jesus. It takes a more intelligent and wise human being to know how to express themselves without the use of perverse communication. Stop using Apostle Peter's weakness to justify your weakness and use of profane communication.

> ▸ Matthew 26:74; Exodus 20:7; Leviticus 19:12;
> Proverbs 10:32; Ecclesiastes 12:9–10; Malachi 2:6–8;
> Ephesians 4:29–30; Colossians 3:8.

421. Avoid inordinate sexual behavior at all costs! You that support the ministry should be just as diligent in behaving yourself wisely as your leader. What you do can affect the whole church. Don't embarrass your family, church, your leader, and most of all, Jesus Christ. If you want respect as a deacon, board member, assistant pastor or head auxiliary officer, then behave yourself wisely! Live so that others will testify of a spirit of excellence in you.

> ▸ Galatians 5:19–21; Ephesians 4:17–30, 5:1–10; Daniel 6:3;
> Jude 1:4; Colossians 3:5; 1 Thessalonians 4:7, 5:22.

422. Be aware that all vices should be avoided! Addictions such as smoking, drinking, drugs, sex, gambling, filthiness of the flesh will ruin your witness and bring reproach to the office you hold! If you are engaging in these things, it is because you have not yet been delivered from a nature of carnality. You may hold a position, but you are as one who is rendering polluted service unto the Lord! You can however bring dignity back to the office you hold and give glory back to God when you stop being in denial, confess, ask the Lord's forgiveness, have a talk with your leader and receive godly, loving counseling and restoration, in Jesus Name!

> ▸ Romans 6:23, 11:29; 2 Chronicles 7:14;
> Joshua 7:19–25; Psalm 34:18; 2 Corinthians 7:10;
> Ephesians 4:17–30, 5:1–10; Jude 1:4–24; 1 John 1:8–10.

423. By the way, how is your behavior? Just because you have a position does not mean that the Lord or His people are going to put up with sin or bad behavior. Make sure that your life is one that truly emulates the life of Christ and the leadership of the old patriarchs.

> ▸ 1 Chronicles 19:13; 1 Corinthians 13:1–5;
> 2 Corinthians 7:1–2, 13:5; 1 Thessalonians 2:10.

424. Cover and support your leader through fasting, prayer, and honest work.

> ▸ Matthew 6:17–18, 18:19–20;
> Acts 4:28–31, 12:5, 12, 13:2–5, 14:23;
> 1 Corinthians 6:5.

425. Never seek to undermine the Lord, your leader, or the ministry. Whatever your role is in the church, be sure to glorify God by fulfilling it.

> ▸ Colossians 3:12–25, 4:17; 1 Samuel 15:22–23;
> Acts 5:29; Jeremiah 42:6.

426. Support and protect the vision. You may not be the foundation of the church, but you can always be a pillar.

> ▸ Ephesians 4:16; Revelation 3:12.

Sack Six
REFINING THE MINISTERS OF MUSIC

(Musicians, praise and worship leaders, choir directors, singers)

427. Are you saved and sanctified, and have you received the baptism of the Holy Ghost? If your answer is "no," then you should read no further. You are living beneath your privilege if you have not accepted Jesus as your personal savior. Invite Him into your life right now! If your answer was "yes," then move on to the next fragment.

> ▶ John 3:16–17; Acts 1:8, 19:1–6; 2 Chronicles 5:11.

428. Reconciliation and repentance when necessary should be done before you operate in your calling or your gift.

> ▶ Romans 11:29; Acts 2:38, 3:19;
> 2 Chronicles 7:14; Hebrews 12:1; 1 John 1:8–10.

429. Are you thoroughly convinced of this gift, calling, or appointment? The Spirit of the Lord will make it plain and confirm it.

> ▶ 1 Samuel 16:23; 1 Chronicles 9:29–33, 15:16–22.

430. Pray that your life is your first original living testimony and your best song!

> ▶ Revelation 12: 11; Psalm 28:7, 40:3, 51:14, 77:6, 104:33–34;
> Isaiah 51:11.

431. Pray for the anointing!

> ▶ Isaiah 10:27; 1 Samuel 16:13–18; 1 John 2:27.

432. Remember your primary responsibility is to glorify God and edify His people.

> ▶ Psalm 68:25, 149–150; Isaiah 42:12;
> 2 Chronicles 5:11–14.

433. Never behave in any manner to take glory from God! No matter how gifted you are, all glory goes to Him!

> ▶ Acts 12:21–23; Ecclesiastes 5:1–6; Psalm 101:1–2;
> 1 Corinthians 13:4–8, 14:33; 1 Chronicles 16:29;
> 2 Chronicles 5:11–14.

434. Never operate in your gift, calling or appointment without first reading God's Word, and praying in order to get an understanding of the gift and how He wants it to be used.

> ▶ Proverbs 3:5–7; 1 Samuel 16:16–23;
> 2 Chronicles 7:14; 2 Timothy 3:16;
> 1 Timothy 4:12–16; Romans 11:29, 12:1–2.

435. Utilizing fasting and prayer will cause there to be "less of you and more of the Lord" as you serve. The Lord will truly be glorified!

> ▶ Joel 2:12–13; John 3:30; Luke 18:1.

436. Are you doing this because you have a gift and desire to obey God or just doing it for hire? Are you dedicated?

> ▶ Job 7:2; Matthew 20:8–13; 1 Chronicles 9:33;
> 2 Chronicles 15:14–22; 1 Timothy 4:14; 2 Timothy 1:6.

437. If you are doing it for hire, then remember this is the Lord's business; respect and honor Him and those who have hired you. Complete the job requested, receive your pay, and avoid being entangled with any other business of the church.

> ▶ Job 7:2; 1 Chronicles 9:33; John 10:10–14.

438. Avoid coercing leaders and their churches into paying you more money than they can afford. Some might call it a form of "extortion."

> ▶ Ezekiel 22:12; Luke 3:13; Proverbs 16:8, 22:16, 28:8.

439. Remember that you are not the pastor.

> ▶ John 10:10–14.

440. Respect the pastor's wishes and/or instructions.

> ▶ Hebrews 13:7, 17.

441. Be on time! Services should not have to be held up to wait for singers or musicians. Someone anointed should go forth and sing a cappella (without instrumental accompaniment) if they must! Do not hinder the service of the Lord! If you have no justifiable reason for consistent tardiness, then it might help for you to occupy a seat and pray while you are learning better stewardship of the Lord's time.

> ▶ Ecclesiastes 3:1, 17, 10:18; Psalm 102:11;
> Matthew 25:1–11; Luke 14:11; 1 Peter 5:5–8;
> Romans 12:11; Hebrews 6:12; Proverbs 18:9.

442. Never take choir members with you to personal appointments unless it has been approved by the pastor of that ministry, especially when they are on duty to serve. They are God's people, but are under the assigned shepherd of that flock.

> ▶ Romans 6:17–18, 8:9–14; 1 Corinthians 15:33;
> Exodus 34:12; 1 John 2:10.

443. Respect the church's style or type of music. Prayerfully question whether the music you are ministering fits into a category of <u>*Worship and Praise*</u>, <u>*war and victory*</u>, or just plain secular, <u>*worldly revelry*</u>! Do not serve in a music department to entertain! You are there to glorify the Almighty God! The church is not an entertainment venue; it is where God's people come together to Worship! They should not have to ask musicians and singers to "take them to church!" We are the church! Your gift, coupled with our worship should invoke the Spirit of the Lord to come and inhabit us (collectively) wherever and whenever we come together as one. When this takes place, then evil spirits will be driven out and true fellowship will have taken place! Therefore, avoid presenting music that can appear to be as "strange fire" (secular, ungodly music) into the worship services of the Lord!

> ▶ John 4:24; Psalm 29:2, 33:2–3;
> Leviticus 10:1–3; 2 Chronicles 5:11–14, 20:22;
> Exodus 15:1–20, 32:16–26; 1 John 2:15;
> 1 Chronicles 25:3; Ephesians 5:19–21; 1 Peter 2:9.

444. Pray about the music including song choices and instruments needed for accompaniment. Question yourself and those in charge: "Will this glorify God?" These choices are important because they are used in the glorification of God. Instruments such as the harp were even used in Old Testament times to accompany prophecy.

> ▶ 1 Chronicles 15:22, 25:1–7; 1 Samuel 10:5–12;
> Proverbs 3:5–6; Ecclesiastes 7:5; Ephesians 5:19–21.

445. Sanctify yourself and receive the anointing so that you can operate in your gift of music effectively as a songwriter, teacher, director, musician or singer. One that is consecrated, humble, and anointed has the potential to invoke the "Cloud" or the "Shekinah" glory of God. When the Shekinah is present, no flesh will be able to stand in the presence of a Sovereign God!

> ▶ John 4:24; 2 Chronicles 5:11–14; Exodus 40:34–37;
> Psalm 16:11; 1 Kings 8:10–11; Isaiah 6:1–7.

446. Treat members and heads of all auxiliaries with the utmost respect including the youth leaders. Everyone deserves respect regardless of their age or gender.

> ▶ 2 Timothy 2:24; Hebrews 10:24–25, 12:14.

447. Remember: the only one with celebrity status is Jesus!

> ▶ John 12:32; 2 Corinthians 4:5.

448. Again: Praise and Worship is all about Jesus and not about you. Your primary purpose is not to entertain but to **lead** God's people in worship. In order for you to do this effectively you must know how to worship God and praise Him for His mighty acts yourself. It would be hard for you to lead His people in something you have never experienced.

> ▶ Ephesians 6:6; John 4:24, 12:42–47; Colossians 3:23.

449. Leave selfishness on the altar. Remember, the body of Christ has many members and not just you by yourself; you can be replaced!

> ▶ 2 Timothy 3:2–9; Philippians 2:2–4;
> Proverbs 25:6–7; Isaiah 14:13–15; Matthew 23:12;
> Luke 22:24–27; 1 Samuel 15:26–28, 18:6–15.

450. Please dress appropriately for rehearsals and meetings as well as for worship service! This includes personal hygiene and no tight, seductive, or revealing clothing, and ripped or torn jeans. Make sure that you can move about in your clothing freely without exposing yourself. If your attire cannot endure the postures of worship, prayer and praise, then do not wear it when you are serving in ministry. Use wisdom! Respect the place of worship and avoid offending His people. Primarily, do not destroy your witness of Christ!

> ▶ Philippians 4:5–8; Galatians 5:18–23;
> 1 John 2:7–16; 1 Timothy 2:8; Hebrews 12:1;
> Nehemiah 8:6; 1 Peter 3:4; 2 Chronicles 5:12–14;
> Psalm 63:4, 95:6, 119:143.

451. Do not compete with the other musicians or singers by performing ridiculously loud! An exception to the rule would be a different type of music. For example, a Christian Rock or Heavy Metal Band, or perhaps in making a *joyful noise* unto the Lord, would be reasons to sing or play loudly. Still, the object is to play in unison (as one voice), so that together everyone can participate and enjoy worshipping God.

However, consider those with sensitive ears whose hearts are often yearning for just a soft, sweet melody.

> ▸ 2 Chronicles 5:13; 1 Corinthians 14:7–8, 10;
> 1 Corinthians 14:15–17; Psalm 68:25;
> Nehemiah 12:42b; 1 Samuel 16:16–18; Genesis 4:21.

452. Remember that as a musician, you are there to accompany the singers and not to drown them out.

> ▸ Psalm 68:25; Ezekiel 33:32; 2 Chronicles 5:13.

453. Never start rehearsals, meetings, or services without prayer; you need God's help! Pray that all meetings and rehearsals be handled in a manner of excellence as well as praying for the anointing and the manifestation of gifts.

> ▸ 2 Chronicles 7:14; Matthew 7:7; Luke 18:1; Proverbs 3:5–6.

454. Learn to find people's strengths as well as their gifts and utilize those who humble themselves before God to receive an anointing from Him while you give them a chance to operate in their gift.

> ▸ 1 Samuel 16:14–23.

455. Never bully anyone! This behavior is highly unacceptable! No laughing, mocking, humiliating or making a spectacle of anyone, their abilities, or the lack thereof.

> ▸ 2 Timothy 3:1–9; 2 Kings 2:23–24; 2 Chronicles 36:16;
> Colossians 4:6.

456. Keep your opinions of others to yourself unless they are solicited; always use constructive criticism prayerfully and only when needed.

> ▸ Matthew 7:1–5; Romans 14:4; 1 Corinthians 4:5;
> Acts 18:25–26; Colossians 4:6.

457. Avoid showing partiality and favoritism.

> ▸ James 2:1–9; Job 13:1–10.

458. Be willing to teach, whenever needed, according to the leading of the Holy Spirit.

> ▸ 1 Chronicles 15:22; 1 Corinthians 14:7–8.

459. Respect diversity in music and prayerfully listen for the anointing in all cultures of music. Make every person feel welcome to be a part of your music ministry. Teach others as well as learn from them. Allow the Holy Spirit to guide you.

> ▸ 1 Corinthians 14:15–17; Daniel 7:14; Philippians 2:10–11.

460. Acknowledge, accept, and welcome every culture of music within your ministry; this is a foreshadowing of the congregation in heaven.

> ▸ Revelation 7:9–17; Philippians 2:9–11;
> 1 Corinthians 12:23–25.

461. Minister to the souls of men, women, boys and girls, and not to their flesh.

> ▸ Jeremiah 31:12–14; Exodus 32:1–25;
> Romans 13:14; Galatians 5:16–21; 1 Peter 4:1–5.

462. Welcome the music of every age group in each ministry. Your choices of music should bless the elderly as well as the youth.

> ▸ Jeremiah 31:12–14; Psalm 67:3–4, 71:9, 107:32, 149:1–3;
> Proverbs 22:6; 1 Chronicles 25:5–7; Ephesians 5:19;
> Nehemiah 12:46; Matthew 19:13–15, 21:15–16; Luke 18:15–16.

463. Take care of the instruments, whether they belong to you, the church, or someone else. Make sure they are maintained, tuned and/or adjusted, and secured when not in use. Do not abuse the instruments just because they don't belong to you. No one, including adults, parents or responsible youth leaders should allow unsupervised, unruly children to destroy God's instruments nor God's house!

> ▸ Numbers 3:8, 4:12; 1 Chronicles 23:5.

464. Discuss needs with your leader when necessary. Consult with them about problems, new ideas, personal issues, and concerns about absent or unruly members as it relates to the music ministry.

> ▸ Hebrews 13:7, 16–17.

465. Carry out all rehearsals and meetings in a timely fashion and with the peace of God.

> ▸ Proverbs 18:9; 1 Corinthians 14:40;
> Romans 12:11; Ecclesiastes 5:1–2.

466. Be vigilant and avoid wounding God's people in the work of the Lord. Meetings and rehearsals can be a time and place where many can get hurt. Never allow anyone to leave your rehearsals, meetings, or services offended without you as a leader trying to get to the root of the problem and advocating peace, and resolution.

> ▸ Matthew 18:6–10; James 3:1–18; Hebrews 12:14;
> Psalm 55:12–13; Proverbs 18:14.

467. Never allow anyone to depart from the ministry without notifying your leader or pastor and allowing them to resolve any underlying issues. The most important thing is "a soul." Never be guilty of running souls (God's people) away from the church.

> ▸ Matthew 18:1–17; Ezekiel 34:6; Psalm 56:8;
> Psalm 55:12–13; Proverbs 27:8; Psalm 119:10.

468. Do not plot and scheme and end up undermining the will of the Lord, your leader, nor the ministry. Whatever your role in the church is, commit to it and glorify God by fulfilling it. Fulfill your responsibilities in a spirit of excellence. Stay in your lane (mind your business and leave others alone)!

> ▸ Colossians 3:12–25, 4:17; Hebrews 10:36;
> Romans 12:2; Ephesians 4:21–30;
> 1 Thessalonians 5:14–22; 1 John 2:15–17.

469. ALERT! Avoid all vices! Addictions, such as smoking, drinking, drugs, sex, and gambling will ruin your witness and could destroy your gift, such as losing your singing voice! Engaging in these activities reveal that you are still yet of a carnal mind. You will continue to struggle with these things until you admit that you have a problem and ask the Lord to deliver you. You may have a gift, but your flesh is putting that gift in jeopardy. You are not operating out of a clean heart and spirit, and therefore it is as if your gift is being offered as strange fire, or a polluted sacrifice! However, deliverance will manifest with true confession, repentance, and obedience to the Word of God. Take the time to receive tender, loving counseling and prayer from your leader. Time off from operating in our gifts is also beneficial towards restoration.

> ▶ Romans 6:12–23, 8:5–7, 11:29; Psalm 34:18;
> 2 Corinthians 7:10; Galatians 5:16–21;
> Ephesians 4:17–30, 5:1–10; 1 Corinthians 5:1–5;
> 1 John 1:7–10.

470. By the way, how is your behavior? This might be a good time for an "on-the-spot check."Right, now, begin to take self-inventory. Just because you have a gift does not mean that you are accepted of the Lord or that His people are comfortable with you as His disciple. When you are operating in your gift, do they feel the love of Jesus as you minister? Make sure that your life is one of the truest, melodious sounds of the Gospel that could ever be sung.

> ▶ 1 Chronicles 19:13; Romans 11:29;
> 1 Corinthians 11:28, 13:3–5; Psalm 101:2;
> 1 Timothy 3:15; 1 Thessalonians 2:10; Ecclesiastes 7:5.

Sack Seven
REFLECTIONS OF GOLD

"Fill this sack with your own personal notes of Wisdom and Word"

Reflections of Gold

Reflections of Gold

About The Authors

"But in a great house there are not only vessels of gold and of silver, but also of wood and of earth; and some to honour, and some to dishonour. "If a man therefore purges himself from these, he shall be a vessel unto honour, sanctified, and meet for the master's use, and prepared unto every good work." —2 Timothy 2:20–21

KAREN J. BUTLER

Karen J. Butler is the founder and pastor of Wings of Deliverance Transforming Ministries in Lincoln Park, Michigan. She has served in the church for fifty years, of which several were spent in Union Baptist Temple, Bridgeton, New Jersey, under the leadership of Rev. Robert W. Davis. It was under his leadership in her younger years that she served as an usher on the Junior Usher Board, became a lead soloist on both the Junior Choir and Choir 2, and was trained to serve as an assistant church secretary at the age of 15.

After having strayed for a time from godly teaching, she turned from sin and completely rededicated her life to the Lord. In 1975 Karen joined Bethel Pentecostal Church in Bridgeton, New Jersey, which is a branch of the Mt. Sinai Holy Churches of America Inc. under the late Bishop Ruth E. Satchell. It was there in February of 1976 that she accepted her call to ministry, preached her initial sermon, and received her ministerial license.

Karen received her evangelist license after continuing to minister at home and across the country. Another of her accomplishments includes a nomination in 1986 as one of "America's Most Outstanding Young Women." Later, in accordance to the rules of the governing hierarchy of her church, she served thirteen years "as an evangelist" before her ordination as an Elder by the Mt. Sinai Holy Churches of America Board of Presbyters in 1989. In that same year she was elected president of the National Youth Convention of Mt. Sinai Holy Churches of America, Incorporated, and served two terms in that position.

Her thirty-seven years of preaching and teaching experience has been in the domestic and foreign field: in cities across the United States, South America, and the Caribbean. She has ministered to God's people through prayer meetings, revivals, seminars, and outreach missions in churches, youth gatherings, street meetings, private homes, nursing homes, and prisons. She currently serves on a panel of pastors on the TCT Network show *Ask the Pastor,* which airs on station WDWO-TV 18 Detroit.

Her fifty years of experience in music includes serving as a choir member, choir director, lead soloist, praise and worship leader, songwriter and musician, as she learned to play the violin at age forty-four. She recorded a demo CD in 2007 titled **There's A Fire in My Soul**, which can be found online at: www.cdbaby.com/cd/karenjbutler

In November 2006, after accepting the call of shepherd and having the first fishnet service, Elder Butler became the founder of **Wings of Deliverance Transforming Ministries**, where she currently serves as pastor. Two years later she experienced a brief challenge of homelessness, while continuing to minister to God's people. Sustained by His grace, in 2010 she started her first semester as a student at Wayne County Community College. She loves God and His people with her whole heart and seeks to be a blessing to all.

> If you are homeless or want to donate, check online
> for local churches, state or city government resources.
> In areas of Michigan go to: www.christ-net.org
> or Grace Centers of Hope—Pontiac, MI

BISHOP JOHNNY BRICE

Saved since 1967 at the tender age of ten, **Bishop Johnny Brice** was called into the ministry of preaching the gospel in 1975 while serving as a member of the Church of God In Christ, Inc. He has been involved in full–time ministry since 1987 in roles that include preaching, singing, teaching; and witnessing at outdoor street meetings, revivals, tent crusades, nursing homes, jails, and prisons. Bishop is the founder of the Miracle Temple Church of Deliverance, Inc. in Detroit, Michigan, where he served as pastor for seventeen years. He is also founder and presiding prelate of Covenant Partners Fellowship, where he hosts an annual fellowship conference that convenes annually in August. This anointed vessel of God now serves the Body of Christ as "The Evangelizing" Bishop, founder and CEO of Johnny Brice Ministries, Inc. This man of God has also served as president of the National Youth Convention of Mt. Sinai Holy Churches of America, Incorporated.

Among many of his friends and fellow ministers Bishop Brice is endearingly referred to as "the preaching machine." Known for his love of church and the Gospel, many are moved by the passionate delivery of his sermons. His service to others and years of experience have helped to make him the outstanding man of God he is today.

Bishop Brice graduated from Montclair State College in Montclair, New Jersey, with a bachelor of arts in sociology and has since earned credits toward his master of arts in education. Married to his lovely bride, Glenda, for thirty–three years and counting; the couple has been blessed with two wonderful children, Samuel and Arielle.

www.ingramcontent.com/pod-product-compliance
Lightning Source LLC
Chambersburg PA
CBHW060349190426
43201CB00043B/1887